FRANCESCA PRINA

The Story of
ROMANESQUE ARCHITECTURE

PRESTEL
Munich · London · New York

CONTENTS

INTRODUCTION

The period from the 11th century until the middle of the 12th century was one of radical transformation in Europe. It was also a time of frenetic activity. After the anxious passing of the year 1000, predicted to be the end of human history, the continent experienced a sense of relief and renewal. Relationships were rekindled; economies and cultures thrived. Agriculture was modernised, with a visible increase in cultivated areas, while crop yields improved due to better tools and triennial crop rotation. Urban areas grew dramatically, accompanied by population growth and a new political and social climate.

Romanesque art and architecture provides evidence of this lively period, during which styles were remarkably similar despite the vast area and range of cultures. Indeed, following many decades of division and war, western Europe gained a renewed sense of communal identity, distinct from both Orthodox Christianity and even Islam. By 1000, the Islamic world, free of Christian millennial superstitions, had already achieved more sophisticated standards of technology and civilisation than in western Europe, and had spread into Mediterranean areas, including Sicily and much of Spain. Some major developments underlined this new sense of identity. Firstly, the Great Schism of 1054 irrevocably divided the church of the Roman Empire into western and eastern branches. Secondly, an improved network of roads led to the increased circulation of goods and ideas. Thirdly, the desire to eliminate the "infidel" from the Holy Land led to the start of the Crusades. And lastly, the revival of secular public culture followed the foundation of the first universities, in Bologna, for example.

One rather widespread and simplified view of the Romanesque style claims that it was most prevalent in rural and isolated parishes: small, mystical and bare churches in the country. As this introduction will demonstrate, however, Romanesque architecture produced some magnificent, complex and large-scale edifices across Europe, from Britain, Germany, France and Spain to Italy and even Scandinavia. In fact, its robustness – based on sculptural forms and principles of the styles of antiquity – aimed to provide a sense of security, solidity and power. Romanesque buildings embody the ideas and aspirations of the Holy Roman Empire, the Church and the city, the three main elements on which European history hinged at the start of the second millennium.

European politics at the time were shaped by the Holy Roman Empire, founded by Charlemagne at the start of the 9th century and revived by German emperors as an administrative structure for central Europe. German

Interior of the Abbey Church of Notre Dame, Bernay, France, circa 1015

One of the earliest examples of Romanesque architecture in Normandy, this long forgotten church is still of interest thanks to some innovative features that became standard elements of Anglo-Norman Romanesque architecture.

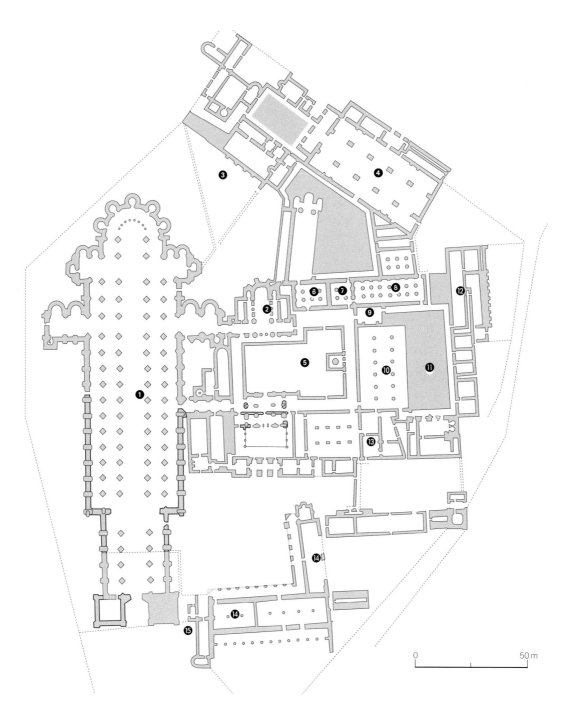

**Diagramatic plan of
Cluny Abbey, France**

(1) 3rd abbey church (Cluny III)
(2) Apse, 2nd abbey church (Cluny II)
(3) Cemetery
(4) Infirmary
(5) Cloister
(6) Chapter house
(7) *Parlatorium*

(8) Monks' dormitory
(9) Calefactory
(10) Refectory
(11) Novices cloister
(12) Lavatories
(13) Kitchen
(14) Hospice for the elderly
(15) Entrance foyer

cathedrals from this period were built according to a "two-headed plan", with two opposite choirs: one for the religious authority (the bishop), and the other for the civil authority (the emperor). Parallel to the foundation of the empire came a reaffirmation of the political and spiritual power of the Church in Rome, with the Pope at its centre; "on the ground", the church maintained its presence through eiscopal seats and abbeys. The Church also underwent reforms in this period, one consequence of which was the expansion of monastic orders. Alongside the traditional rule of St Benedict, who focused on the motto "ora et labora" (pray and work), the nascent Cistercian order experienced a rise at the beginning of the 12th century. The great abbeys developed into political and economic centres across medieval Europe, located in protected – often fortified – complexes structured like small, self-sufficient enterprises where piety and industry went hand in hand. They managed large tracts of land and generated vast revenues, which in turn drove their growth into sizeable local and regional powerhouses. The church portals, decorated capitals, choir stalls, furnishings, relics and reliquaries all represented the "high" art of the Romanesque in Europe. One of the most famous examples of such a place is the Cluny Abbey in France, which grew to impressive proportions. Even the mere fragments that remain provide visible testimony to the sheer magnificence of the original building.

Following a revival of commerce at the start of the 11th century, many cities, especially those that held regular markets and were able to trade free of duty or taxes, witnessed a dramatic process of urban and economic development. The major urban centres of Europe began demanding substantial autonomy from their distant emperor, as did the episcopal seats, which, though still under nominal control of the Pope, effectively became local centres of religious authority during this period.

Romanesque, romance and Roman: a new era and the commemoration of antiquity

The term "Romanesque" was coined by French medievalists and archaeologists at the beginning of the 19th century to define the major characteristics of the new civilisation of 11th- and 12th-century western Europe – and to distinguish it from earlier revivals witnessed in imperial art during the Carolingian and Ottonian eras (8th–10th centuries) and from art of the later Gothic period (late 12th–14th centuries). The term Romanesque, which evokes the contemporary reference to "Romance" literature and language with a common "root" in Latin, also underpinned one of the distinctive principles of the new style: a common reference to classical methods and models of construction, albeit with different regional forms. The rediscovery of Roman techniques and the reuse of ancient Roman materials began at this time across the main regions of Europe, with some local variation. It is important, however, to distinguish here between architectural "remains" or "fragments" – physically lifted from their ancient location and reused in new sites – and Romanesque examples where new materials were used to produce architectural components according to classical styles, motifs or themes.

In the High Middle Ages, the reuse of antique building materials was primarily a means to save time and labour; in Romanesque architecture, the recycling was more selective. The spoils were put on display in prominent positions for their aesthetic as well as political significance. In medieval architecture, in fact, many religious buildings are constructed in part with marble recovered

opposite page
Ground plan of Cluny Abbey, France, circa 1157

This abbey complex, unlike the church, comprised a vast and not very orderly ensemble of buildings, partly adapted to monastic life and partly used for agricultiural activities and secular purposes for centuries before it was dismantled after the French Revolution. It is a fascinating example of a fixed social order. After being rebuilt three times, few of its original architectural elements remain, but some sculptures and capitals from the choir are displayed in a museum on the site. The rather geometric plan of the 3rd church (Cluny III) includes five naves, a double transept to add capacity, a choir and ambulatory, radial chapels, a large narthex (a porticoed atrium where catechumens and penitents approach the entrance to the sacred building) and multiple towers.

Capital in the Corinthian style, Modena Cathedral, Italy, 11th/12th centuries

At the end of the 11th century, the "ancient" Corinthian capital experienced a revival in monumental Romanesque architecture, good examples of which are the capitals in the nave at Modena Cathedral. These capitals became the main features of imitation and emulation in medieval workshops.

Florence Baptistery, Italy, 1070–1230

Architects from central Italy, who had contact with Roman remains, tended to favour ancient Roman styles. The Florence Baptistery was inspired by ancient models, its exterior revealing a complex geometric organisation and the development of three classical orders.

from ancient Roman sites, whether in structural elements, such as columns, or in decorative elements. The reclamation not only had practical purposes but also ideological ones; it was an attempt to reconstruct "classical" surroundings as evidence of continuity with the grandeur of ancient Roman times.

Typical examples of the reclamation of materials from that epoch are columns and capitals. They were easy to unearth, transport and reposition. In the Romanesque period, columns from demolished ancient buildings were often reused in churches, palaces or bell towers as well as for long cloister arcades, in furnishing décor for windows and doorways, or for interior decorative schemes such as niches and canopies. The phenomenon is certainly not rare, especially in the areas most heavily influenced by Rome, namely Italy, France and Spain, and it served as a symbol of links with Rome, perceived from many perspectives as the historic origin of the Empire, an icon of classical values, the cradle of Christianity and a symbol of the triumph of the Roman Catholic Church in Europe.

The site and the architect

Medieval urban development and the construction of new cathedrals was the product of an elaborate collective effort by architects, patrons, master builders and all the specialists necessary to make a project of such scope a reality. The Romanesque building site was a complex place that included the organisation of labour, the collection and transport of building materials, the arrangement of work around climatic conditions and seasons, and the coordination of different phases of construction.

The Romanesque building site remained essentially anonymous and rather resembled a choral "unison", due to the supervision by master builders working in teams and due to its status as a product of the community's economic and ideological commitment. Within this anonymity, however, it is possible to identify some specialist artisans.

Among the tradesmen was a group of builders, stonemasons and sculptors known as the "Comacine masters" (from Comacina Island in Lake Como) that travelled around Europe erecting Romanesque cathedrals and other great works of architecture and architectural decoration. Documented as early as the 7th century, and originating in the valleys between Italy and Switzerland, especially the area near Lake Lugano and Lake Como, the Comacine masters were organised in teams able to set up and carry out enterprises on a vast scale, thanks to advanced technologies and a superbly organised work schedule. The output of these Lombard master builders was founded on common stylistic principles that produced a high degree of homogeneity in Romanesque cathedrals across Italy and beyond, starting with prototypes such as the Basilica of Sant'Ambrogio in Milan. Some of the most recognisable motifs among these were the triangular gables on cathedral façades, the small blind arches decorating the upper portions of those façades and the increasing size of the openings in the bell towers, seen from the lower level moving upwards. Additionally, thanks to the "international" output of these master builders and the wide dissemination of their designs and projects, strong analogies can be drawn from the architectural style founded in a number of other territories around 1000 (in abbey complexes as well as in episcopal seats).

On communally organised building sites from the Romanesque period, the architect's persona became indistinguishable from that of the master builder. Given the prevalence of practical over theoretical knowledge, the master builder's training was largely passed down through oral tradition, so-called site practice, even if some builders could read and write and knew geometric rules regarding proportions. With the subsequent emergence of an urban middle class, the role of the person directing architectural work – also called magister, architectus or artifex – changed and required a more specific creative and social element. This is how the growth in the professional status of architects began in communal Italian society in the late 11th century, when a number of important personalities emerged, including Lanfranco, architect of Modena Cathedral, and Buscheto, one of the architects of Pisa's cathedral.

***Lanfranco directing work at Modena Cathedral**, parchment miniature, Modena, Biblioteca Capitolare, 12th century*

This scene was recorded in a codex from the 12th century, when Lanfranco became known as mirabilis artifex mirabilis aedificator (superior builder superior architect). Indeed, contemporary sources leave no doubt regarding the prestige and role enjoyed by the architect. His experience spanned from Lombard tradition to French/German tradition and was expressed with absolute originality in the construction of Modena Cathedral. This image shows the architect's increased social status with Lanfranco shown elegantly dressed with a cloak in one hand and directing proceedings. He is differentiated from the labourers by the inscription as 'operarii e artifices', and by his clothing.

Construction of the Tower of Babel, French Bible, John Rylands University Library, University of Manchester, ms. Fr 5 fol 1, beginning of the 14th century

These iconographic images offer a lively account of the work taking place at large medieval building sites. Not accounting for the elements "recycled" from ancient monuments, building materials were sourced locally due to transportation considerations. After the foundations were laid, the bricklayers, masons and sculptors were followed by plasterers, carpenters and other artisans. From the miniatures, we can see the early use of scaffold-like structures placed around and at the top of the building; they were moved and relocated by hand as work proceeded. Only in the 14th century did wooden structures similar to scaffolds appear. To transport materials to the higher levels they used ramps and pullies with baskets.

Commissioning architectural work

During the Romanesque period, the visual arts were expressed in many different ways, from highly cultivated works to more simplified forms. The Church, for example, was often effectively depicted in illustrated manuscripts, a representation of the culture of its epoch that the faithful could "read" during services (which were held in the vernacular by the 9th century). This largely explains the importance of ecclesiastical bodies in commissioning architectural work starting in the early medieval period. It also explains the huge impact of the Church, not only through what is now defined as a true "campaign of images", used for its powers of persuasion, suggestion and education, but also through its interpretation of the role that the construction of cathedrals had for a community on both a symbolic and material level.

The feverish increase in economic activity from the 11th century resulted in the development of new types of commissions in urban centres. This led to the cathedral becoming not merely a symbol of identity but an icon of urban revival and of the crafts and mercantile activities that supported its construction. At first, the great monasteries performed the function of promoting the new culture, but the cities – new centres of political and economic power – quickly became centres of knowledge and culture as well. A new order thus emerged, in which a separation of secular and religious power, and an affirmation of collective values in the city's social classes and in their civic organisations, stimulated diversification in the placing of commissions. This, in turn, increased cultural and artistic production beyond the powerful stimulus created by the harmless but lively rivalry between city-states. The presence of a bishop and a secular power in one city created healthy competition compared with the limited ecclesiastical and imperial commissioning of the early medieval period. Cathedrals and residential palaces began popping up in city centres, typically around the central squares. They were buildings with strong symbolic value in which bishops and councils of citizens shared responsibilities for spiritual guidance and administrative affairs. The secular nobility also intervened directly in the surrounding rural areas, assuming a political role that included ideological and social propaganda, as shown in the celebratory fresco at the Abbey of Santa Maria di Rovegnano (Chiaravalle), painted centuries after the abbey's construction. In any case, work on a building has been a sign of order and prosperity since ancient times. Furthermore, cities united by common economic interests created leagues as well as political or commercial alliances that were destined to redraw the geography of power, from the epoch of free city-states through to the epoch of "Signorie" governed by the hereditary aristocracy.

A STYLE FOR EUROPE

Alongside the expansionist impulse that made the military resurgence in western Europe possible, the tireless production of works of art and architecture gave rise to the most important legacies of the Romanesque period. Amazing in its sheer scale, the phenomenon was actually so long-lasting and widespread that, according to Rodolfo the Bald, a Cluniac monk in the period just after the year 1000, Europe was dressed up in "a white cloak of churches". Inside those churches, which were sites of both symbolic and tangible importance, all the cultural values of the epoch were given expression. In fact, the images from the period form a sort of encyclopedia of events and movements, captured in the decorative schemes of places of worship, where sacred stories are depicted alongside pagan mythology, allegorical figures and scenes from everyday life. All together, it made up a figurative heritage, recognisable to all, in which the faithful see themselves depicted together with the values they hold so dear.

Romanesque art makes use of many methods that are highly effective in providing a sense of participation in the detailed narrative and shared destiny of so many European nations. The period has a common architectural thread as well as easily recognisable personalities and scenes from the decorative arts. Even while different spoken languages had established themselves around the continent, Latin was adopted as a universal code, not only in the Church but on a wider cultural level. And although Europeans no longer spoke the language of Cicero, medieval works were mostly rendered in Latin, from illuminated scripts to formal inscriptions on churches and monuments.

View of Mont-Saint-Michel, France

The religious architecture of the Romanesque period is characterised by a significant increase in both height and volume that resulted in bell towers, or keeps, of massive dimensions, which in turn gave rise to feelings of awe and subjection. Such architectural structures naturally lent themselves to highly visible and prominent locations. As such, edifices planned like this were more than just symbols of the power of the Church and the Crown; they provided landmarks for travellers and wayfarers as well as sanctuaries for pilgrims on their way to selected destinations. Sanctuaries dedicated to St Michael, for example, were erected throughout the medieval period on hills or high rocks to make the archangel's protective embrace seem tangible by dint of his position; he was also depicted armed, as a conqueror of evil. Elevating the church to the highest point was intended to put worshippers closer to God, and to create an imposing, monumental scene. In this way, Romanesque architecture, deeply rooted in its locations, was very much in harmony with the natural environment. One only needs to think of the Abbey of Mont-Saint-Michel in Normandy, rising above land and water, the Sainte-Foy abbey church in Conques, standing out on a steep slope in the Auvergne, or the Cathedral of Trani in Puglia, whose bell tower stands out like a lighthouse signal for seafarers. In addition to these symbolic functions, architects also had to respond structurally to shifting liturgical needs (with an increasing number of altars), to pilgrimages, to the cult of relics and to religious processions that wound their way through the inside and outside of the sacred sites. The large number of examples from the period between 1000 and 1250 are fascinating in their contrast, from the purity of the overall design to the infinite variations of that very theme due to the choice

below
Sacra di San Michele, Turin, Italy, 12th century

In Italy, as in France, churches dedicated to St Michael were built in elevated positions so they would be visible from as many angles as possible. On the summit of Mount Pirchiriano, a rocky peak in the Val de Susa, the small complex around this church has dramatic, high walls with embellishments of green stone that contrast beautifully with the grey foundation.

opposite page
Saint Michel d'Aiguilhe, Le Puy-en-Velay, France, 962

The cult of St Michael was one of the most popular in medieval France. The saint was thought to be God's messenger and a victor over Satan. He was also the messenger of Jove (in antiquity), patron saint of pagan Gaul and a focus of general devotion in the area. Saint Michel d'Aiguilhe is built on a basalt peak 85 metres (280 feet) high directly before the city of Le Puy-en-Velay. It has an oratory at the top of 268 steps cut into the rock and the chapel has a bell tower and a circular gallery.

of materials and the arrangements of the sites; and this applied to the grandest monastery complexes or the smallest parish churches and chapels amidst landscapes of rare and remote beauty.

The origins and development of sacred architecture

For practical as well as indisputable reasons of prestige and symbolic quality, Romanesque architecture clearly reconnected itself with the buildings of the ancient Roman Empire by re-employing selected technical methods, such as the single-centred arch, the use of pilasters and the solid system of wall construction. Even the word "duomo", the Italian term for cathedral, derives from the Latin "domus" and stands, in fact, for the grand and secure house of all the faithful, a building built in solid stone, or in brick, that would be safe against fires and natural calamities, and survive in the middle of cities that consisted, for the most part, of timber houses.

Another basic characteristic of Romanesque architecture is its dialogue between the substantial uniformity of style and technique (based on a similarity of function, on models from antiquity and on the fairly consistent cultural preferences of the ruling class), on the one hand, and on the other, a panorama of regional differences, each of rich but varying quality. This polarity is linked to the politics of the time and to the evolution of social

below
St-Étienne, Nevers, France, circa 1063–1097

Nevers is a historic city in western Burgundy, near the River Loire. The Church of St-Étienne is home to a priory linked to the Cluniac Order and is an important Romanesque structure that has been preserved without any alterations. Comparisons have been made with Peterborough Cathedral (opposite) in England due to the importance of the two buildings. The interior at Peterborough is articulated with circular and octagonal pillars, while Nevers has square pillars. The central nave is wide, with matronea (women's galleries) that have double circular arches for openings. The light comes into the area thanks to windows in the clerestory on the upper level of the interior walls. The French example has a barrel-vaulted ceiling far less elaborately decorated than its counterpart in Peterborough. Also, the vault above the choir at Peterborough was done in the Gothic style.

opposite page
Choir, Peterborough Cathedral, UK, 12th century

Churches on three "levels", with matronea and clerestories, are typical of medieval England. They tended to accentuate the height of the women's galleries and walls and multiply the number and thickness of passageways. These elements resulted in the well-lit nave at Peterborough.

structures. Europe was gaining knowledge of its spiritual identity while the
single central political power, that of the Holy Roman Empire, was being
questioned as a result of the rise of feudalism, on the one hand, and of
independent cities on the other. Significant regional differences here trace
their origins beyond the diversity of political and social formations to the
substrata of local cultures. In the creation of these various "languages",
a number of factors come into play: the influence of building and figurative
traditions rooted in certain localities, the reception, readily or otherwise,
of external influences and the employment of local building materials for
construction and sculptural ornament. From the brick of northern Italy and
the marble of Tuscany to the sandstone of Germany and the Istrian stone
of the Adriatic regions, these factors resulted in distinct regional accents
that make use of the intrinsic qualities of different materials and give rise
to the invention of individual structural solutions and various effects of
decoration and colour.

In terms of style, the Romanesque phase of European architecture was a
uniform movement that stretched across most of western Christianity at
the time. This context inspired a variety of artistic scenarios with two
discernible extremes: in south-western Europe, churches vaulted for the first

**Apsidal view of the Basilica
of St Sernin, Toulouse, France,
1060–1150**

Along the Way of St James, which leads to Santiago de Compostela, Spain, a new style of architecture developed in response to the needs of pilgrims. It looked to guarantee the safe passage of thousands of travellers, who came to venerate holy relics along the way. At St Sernin, the presbytery had to be extended to make space for an expanding clergy, to contain the spread of religious rituals around the central altar and to multiply the number of minor altars connected to the cult of holy relics. This led to the revolutionary adoption of a choir with an ambulatory that was dilated by a series of chapels and combined with a transept with lateral naves, four small apses and, above it, a crossing tower. Outside, the perspectival and chiaroscuro effects of each architectural solution translated into a complex and articulated plan, all dominated by a tall central tower, which at many pilgrimage churches made the structure visible from a distance.

time entirely in stone, a technical innovation born with the Romanesque; and in northern and central Europe quite a different architecture featuring large, wide churches with wooden roofs, plentiful light and towers. In the German territories, Imperial power endured such that Carolingian and Ottonian artistic traditions could thrive while in southern regions, and in particular in the Po Valley and in Tuscany, the early rise of self-governing communities created the conditions for a more dynamic and varied form of development. The panorama of Italian Romanesque architecture is markedly different from that of other countries in Europe, especially the variety and originality of the solutions adopted in its different regions. A country open to influences from the Alps and across the sea, the Italian peninsula was home to a figurative language that is distinct in each region and that took on the role of filter for various Mediterranean and oriental influences. The traditions of late antiquity and early Christianity endure and are clearly seen in Florence, Rome and Campania. Venice, like much of southern Europe and the Adriatic region, is more influenced by Byzantine culture, while Lombardy and Emilia appear anchored in a European Romanesque: traditional and novel elements woven in a continual dialogue with results of extraordinary originality. While the cathedral was the most important monument in the cities of the Italian peninsula, it was the abbeys and great churches in France that became the centres of artistic innovation, despite the growth of towns and villages. They were where important relics of saints are preserved and venerated, and they were constructed along pilgrimage routes specifically designed to welcome the faithful in large numbers.

Elsewhere, such as in the kingdoms of northern Spain, the role of local rulers took precedence over the activities of abbeys or religious sanctuaries for pilgrims, thus creating a situation – not dissimilar to southern Italy – of continual exchange with eastern Mediterranean civilisations. Conversely, Normandy, though relatively lean as far as ancient monuments are concerned but very important from a strategic and cultural perspective, saw a rapid military expansion that translated into a powerful building programme promoted by dukes, abbots and bishops that was conceived as a spectacular means of legitimising their power. It is from this diverse context that the rich and varied picture of the Romanesque in Europe emerges. At the moment of its greatest expansion, there were parallel as well as interconnected developments that make it impossible to clearly identify the influence or derivation of one centre from another.

Models and solutions in religious architecture

Romanesque religious buildings represent a complex articulation of space that goes far enough to annul the unified spatial effects and directional continuity of the great churches of preceding epochs. As the different parts of the church are laid out in relation to their uses, individual structural elements are created in response to certain static and spatial requirements. The systems adopted in Romanesque architecture created solid vaulted buildings immune to fire and suited to choir singing. The robust walls came at the cost of windows, which, at the beginning at least, were few and small. In the half-light of

Perspectival drawing of Drübeck Abbey, Drübeck, Germany, begun in 1004

This church has an altar level on two storeys with arched arcades (1) that provide an alternative system of support typical of architecture in this region, namely, pilaster-column-pilaster (2). An ample wall surface extends from here, followed by a clerestory (3). The thickness of the walls emphasises their supportive role, while two levels of stairs lead to the elevated presbytery (4). In most cases, Romanesque churches had a crypt below the presbytery (as seen in earlier examples), where holy relics were collected and preserved.

a Romanesque church, Byzantine models are left behind and the formal language of antiquity is abandoned; the column is replaced by the pilaster and wall surfaces are transformed from insubstantial into thick masses. The wide and smooth wall surfaces, primarily in Italy and in some places in Spain, became the perfect support for the vast fresco cycles. The Romanesque cathedral almost always features a nave and two side aisles terminating in one (or more) semi-circular apse and a large transept that comprises the horizontal arm of an ideal cross. The presbytery, the holiest part of the building, is at the "head" of the cross and is reserved for the clergy. The high altar and bishop's chair are here, and it is often raised above the crypt – this is a major difference from older, early-Christian designs.

One of the main concerns of Romanesque builders was to close the roof with stone vaults, a more stable and safer structure than roofs and beams of timber. To achieve this, architects adopted the barrel vault often used in Roman architecture. Early-Romanesque edifices in Catalonia, Burgundy and Normandy, for example, used this technique, adding so-called groin vaults in the smaller and lower side aisles. The vault formed by the intersection of two barrel vaults formed four segments called "cells" and distributed the weight of the roof to the four corners of the square. To strengthen these four points, cruciform pilasters were placed inside; outside, the structure was reinforced with massive buttresses. Still, for reasons of stability and mass in the curtain walls, openings were reduced to a minimum; the windows are few and narrow along the aisles and in the concave apses.

The requirements imposed by functionial needs – solemn processions, the number of altars needed, cults of relics in crypts, increasing numbers of pilgrims – resulted in the creation of spaces in the church reserved for the

below
Interior of Silvacane Abbey, Provence, France, 1175–1230

If you take away the windows and clerestory from the central nave of a church, thereby eliminating direct light, it is termed a "blind nave". This is what one finds at Silvacane. The only light here comes from the lateral naves. The harmony of proportions, precise angles and simple beauty of the high walls foreshadow a later, more robust version of Cistercian architecture.

officiating clergy. The choir was thus enlarged by the adjacent transept, for example, while a cupola or tower was often placed at the crossing of the nave and transept, symbols of the soul rising toward God. Space in the naves is articulated by a series of supports (columns, squared pilasters or pilasters with a composite profile) that rise up to the vaults and impart the design to each bay (the space defined by the four or six uprights around each compartment). These bays then became the module on which the whole building was planned. The ratio (nearly always 1:2 in both height and width) between the bays of the central nave and the side aisles in turn generated the system of supports alternating between columns and pilasters (the binary method known as "Rhenish") or pilaster-column-column (the tertiary system known as "Saxon"). The great Romanesque churches of continental Europe are articulated in three or four levels: the arches on the lowest order; the matronea (galleries originally for women) running above the side aisles

and looking out on to the central nave; the triforium, an intermediate level of blind arches; and finally by the clerestory, the series of window openings along the length of the highest part of the outer walls. This complex structure is less frequent in German or Italian examples of the Romanesque, where even the most important cathedrals or other great churches such as those in Lombardy or Emilia are limited to only two main levels and are thus somewhat dimly lit inside.

Monasticism

After surviving "the end of times" that were meant to arrive with the year 1000, the 11th century remained a time of strong mystic tension in which the existential principles of monasticism endured. Monks took a leading role in medieval society and their lives were seen as the ultimate expression of genuine Christianity. They were mediators between the earthly and the spiritual, appointed to engage with the forces that governed life and death. To overcome their own fears and establish contact with otherworldly powers, society attributed great importance to formulae and gestures and feared the invisible; it needed rites and sacraments, but required them in tangible, solid and safe buildings; they needed images of a celestial Jerusalem, predicted in the Apocalypse of Saint John the Evangelist as the true home of the just, the mystical "city" that awaited the blessed. The basic duty of monks was to pray for humanity; the monastery was a place for activities that led to collective redemption, an instrument for salvation.

Monasteries grew and became rich not only due to the business of agriculture and endowments directly given to the abbey, but also due to their privileged

relationships with nobility and royalty, who maintained their loyalty with donations of assets and lands in exchange for prayers. To allow monks more time for prayer, significant alterations to Benedictine rule were introduced. Founded in the 6th century on the principle of "ora et labora" (pray and work), the reform imposed daily manual labour and was enforced by the Cluniac Order, which took its name from the abbey in Cluny, France. From then on, monks focused on the liturgical office, with great emphasis placed on choral singing, a splendid rite of continual praise and calls for God's intercession. The privileged position accorded to the abbot (on the central column of the cloister of Moissac, for example) underscores the will of monks to resist an ideal similar to that of the apostles – as "pillars" of a universal church – but also with the role the Cluniacs hoped to assume at the centre of the Church. Hundreds of monasteries thrived throughout Europe; they were cells of faith, tradition, science and culture that greatly influenced the story of medieval architecture. Their function was to justify the use of revenues for works of embellishment and to reflect the glory of God and the radiant image of the celestial city in the grandeur of the buildings and splendour of the arts. However, the magnificence of the architecture and adornments of the Cluniacs at the end of the 11th century gave rise to a heated debate on the "poverty" of the Church in its use of material goods. The Cistercian Order even provided arguments against the "luxury" of the Cluniacs, thanks above all to the leading figure of St Bernard of Clairvaux, a different kind of spiritual role model, who inspired a radical rethinking of the architectural models.

Benedictine monastic architecture

Monasteries were intended as utopian settlements, each structured differently, according to the functions they fulfilled. Since their beginnings in the 6th century, Benedictine foundations were oases of stability and productivity based on an internal organisation of enviable discipline that lived by the rule of "ora et labora" and easily integrated with medieval society. They welcomed young recruits as well as older men hoping to end their days closer to God's warm embrace. Evangelical bases, agricultural powerhouses, and centres of learning and education, monasteries were structured around their great novelty element: the cloister. The architectural heart of all monastery complexes and an integral part of the liturgical routine, cloisters were a symbol of the cosmic order but also a place of prayer, meditation and relaxation. Among the great medieval monastic complexes built according to the Benedictine model, of which hundreds were completed around Europe, Monte Cassino (founded in Italy by St Benedict in the 6th century and rebuilt by Abbot Desiderio in the 11th century), Cluny (founded in Burgundy by William of Aquitaine in 910) and Cîteaux (also founded in Burgundy, in 1098, by Robert de Molesme) stand out. The design of the church and other spaces within the convent were drawn along the sides of the square cloister and based on a centuries-old model derived from the Carolingian original, the Abbey of Saint Gall (9th century), which provided a compact layout that was widely copied in centuries that followed.

Cluny Abbey, France

Founded in 910, the abbey at Cluny represents a pivotal moment in the religious history of Europe. Due to major reforms to the *Rule of St Benedict*,

below
Santa Maria Monastery Church and Bell Tower, Pomposa Abbey, Ferrara, Italy, mid-11th century

The bell tower at Pomposa Abbey is a typical feature of the early Romanesque in Italy: visible from afar, it is considered symbolic of the power of religious communities and towns. The bell tower is the work of a master who signed himself Deusdedit (1063). Divided into nine orders and punctuated by pilasters and blind arches, it gradually becomes lighter towards the top due to the increasing size of the windows.

and the abbey's huge network of branches and affiliations, Cluny quickly became one of the wealthiest and mightiest monasteries in Europe, led by celebrated and esteemed abbots like Peter the Venerable (1120–1130). The reforms ultimately placed the order under the direct control of the Pope, effectively freeing it from the jurisdiction of episcopal and feudal powers and providing monks with a respite from exhausting manual labour in order to dedicate more of their time to prayer, celebration of liturgical offices and ritual processions. Amidst the splendour and solemnity of services, celebrated with sumptuous excess akin to imperial ceremony and reflected in the design and decoration of its vast church, Cluny Abbey provided an opportunity to express magnificence, grandeur and wealth as the primary attributes for offerings to God and the praise of his glory – clearly employing an aesthetic that reflected the importance of the Church and the feudal hierarchies.

In the space of just one century, the main abbey of the Cluniac Order was rebuilt three times to accommodate the new needs of a growing monastic community. The main building was, of course, the abbey's vast basilica, with three naves and a well-developed transept and choir. After its third reconstruction in 1080, it immediately became famous for the grandiosity of its architectural forms: at 171 metres (565 feet) in length, it was the grandest monument of medieval Christianity and the most comprehensive record of the cultural importance of the great abbeys.

St Bernard of Clairvaux

The organisational and structural choices made by St Bernard (1090–1153) signified a clear shift in the history of architecture. In a letter to another monk, Abbot William of Saint Thierry, Bernard described a visit to Cluny in which he elaborated upon each of the ornate cloister capitals individually. In a celebrated and vivid literary passage, he expressed the conflict he experienced between the fascination of the capitals and the distraction they

above left
View of Martin-du-Canigou Monastery, France, 1001–1026

Early-Romanesque buildings in southern Europe are mostly small, sturdy structures with stone vaults and limited natural light.

above right
Cluny Abbey, France, 10th century

The southern arm of the transept is the only surviving fragment of the church here, which was razed around 1810. Its originality lies not only in the extraordinary complexity of the whole, but also in the tendency to accentuate the height of the nave with regard to the width, in a ratio of 1:3; it is an adaptation of the pre-Gothic ogival arch, introducing a system of direct lighting.

presented for a monk trying to focus on prayer: "In the cloisters, where monks devote themselves to holy readings, why are those grotesque monsters intruding with their deformed beauty and their beautiful deformity? What do those filthy monkeys, ferocious lions and bizarre centaurs, who are only half man, signify? Why those spotted tigers? Why warriors in battle? Why hunters blowing their horns? One depicts several bodies with only one head, the other several heads with one body. Over here the tail of a reptile is attached to a quadruped, and over there the body of a quadruped is put on a fish. Another shows an animal riding a horse. Lastly, the images are so varied and incredible that one is compelled to interpret the marble instead of reading manuscripts; one must spend the day looking at these marvels instead of contemplating God's law."

Moreover, Bernard was seriously concerned about the cost of the decorations, about the magnificence of the goldsmiths' work, and about the use of Church income for the decoration of Church architecture instead of helping the poor, for example. In order to instill a degree of purity in prayer, choral singing and productive activity, St Bernard sought a return to the basics, to simple forms, straight lines, squares and cubes. As a result, a "rationalistic" architectural practice came to dictate the construction of abbeys. Useless ornamentation was barred and the centre was no longer the church but the cloister, a mystical location and the heart of every monk's universe. The cloister had four galleries, akin to the four seasons, four elements, four continents and four points of the compass. Cistercian architecture, for its part, seeks light. The course of the sun dictated the orientation of the areas where particular daily activities took place around the cloister, which provides access to all the buildings: the chapter house, the refectory, the

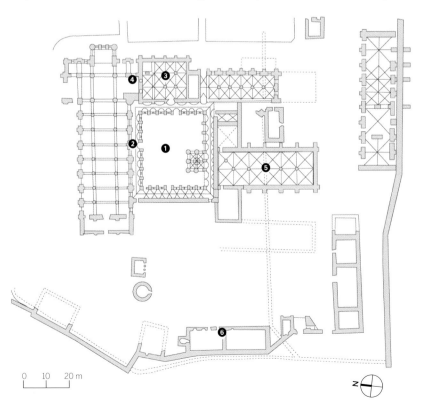

0   10   20 m

N

Plan of the Abbey of Fontenay, France, circa 1147

The architectural model of Cistercian monasteries remained more or less unchanged throughout the Middle Ages, adhering to the plan outlined by St Bernard of Clairvaux and based on that of the Abbey of St Gall (9th century). The monks' living, meeting and working quarters are arranged along three sides of the cloister arcade (1) while the fourth side (2) – generally the northern – is closed off and protected by the body of the church. The chapter house (3), where the monks held meetings, is on the eastern side, as is the dormitory on the floor above, with stairs providing direct access from the transept (4) of the church. To the south are the kitchens and the refectory (5), while the western wing houses the monastery services and the entrance (6).

dormitory, the abbot's apartment and, most importantly, the church, where no stained glass, with its artificial and impure colours, was allowed to obscure or modify the transparent clarity of sunlight, a metaphor for God's love, a spiritual staircase that the saintly monk climbs, totally absorbed by this vision.

From the village to the city

From the 11th century onwards, the layout of non-religious settlements was determined by a series of building types, including a castle, a watchtower and a city encircled by walls, all of them organised in a reciprocal manner. In fact, the increase in agricultural production and overall population completely transformed the relationship between town and country. Across Europe – in Italy and in the Netherlands before anywhere else – urban centres began experiencing very rapid growth; ancient cities were revived and new ones were founded, typically in locations where frequent markets were held.

The Romanesque city generally had a circular, enclosed layout with an irregular street plan protected by walls that isolated it from the surrounding countryside. Apart from being one of the most burdensome economic projects the population undertook in order to defend its autonomy, the walls also represented the perimeter to which city laws extended, thereby differentiating the residents of the city from those in the country. This, in turn, kept the latter bound into feudal submission by a squire and tied to the land on which they laboured. Beneath the tall outlines of bell towers and buildings that rose above residential areas, the city basically organised itself around the church and the market, where the majority of social and commercial activity took place. The city, thus configured, became a centre for the exchange of products that flowed in from the countryside, a hub for crafts and trading, and a major junction in a network of roads upon which not only manufactured goods and primary materials travelled, but also news and cultural developments. It was in these urban centres that a new middle class developed, whose activity not only greatly complemented agricultural production, but also inspired the process of profound trans-formation that took place in medieval society.

Interior of the Abbey of Fontenay, France, circa 1147

Built under St Bernard of Clairvaux's direction, Fontenay is modelled on the blind nave churches of southern Europe and applies the principles of the order's founder. The simple but massive nave is deep and spanned by a tunnel vault cut by transverse arches; it is a long, uninterrupted single volume with beams of light entering only from the side bays and high windows, a strictly geometric architectural solution used by the Cistercians throughout Europe.

View of Monteriggioni, Siena, Italy, 13th century

Built in the 13th century by the Sienese to counter the expansion of Florence, this fortified village reflects the strategy Italian towns used to protect their territories from attempted encroachment by rival neighbours. The restoration of the battlements was accompanied by the foundation of new settlements with both military and civic purposes. The result of this dominance of cities over the surrounding countryside was the proliferation of smaller towns scattered densely around northern-central Italy.

Vernacular architecture

While religious architecture represented the main focus in medieval construction activities, the importance of civic and military architecture should not be completely overlooked. Typical of the feudal era, castle settlements were effectively expanded by parceling out land, which was then managed alternatively by the civic authorities or by individual feudal overlords. Monumental defensive structures thus developed in the countryside, mainly near strategic points for the purpose of controlling a specific area; these fortified cities and citadels unified both residential and defensive functions. In settlements surrounded by city walls and fortifications, and where individual homes did not need to perform defensive functions, a trend of decorating façades began to develop. It included sophisticated arches, galleries and mullioned, double-paned windows. The exteriors of Romanesque palaces, for example, are particularly polished as a result, even in the absence of any sculptural embellishments.

The construction of private residences intensified as the middle classes became wealthier. In built-up and densely populated urban areas, residences grew upward and were often equipped with cellars in which, when possible, builders capitalised on the foundations of pre-existing Classical buildings. With the increase of civil liberties came the ever greater importance of city halls and public administration buildings. The standard of living gradually increased as well, despite poor hygienic conditions, the scarcity of running water and a total absence of buildings dedicated to sport, culture and theatre. Indeed, for several centuries to come, the ruins of Roman baths,

View of Vézelay, France

This small town was built atop an isolated hill on the Morvan Plains on one of the routes leading to Santiago de Compostela in Spain. Vézelay's urban growth was dictated by the restrictions of its site: the buildings crowd around the bulk of the Basilica of St Mary Magdalene, which occupies much of the available space.

circuses, amphitheatres and other theatres served no greater purpose than as open-air quarries for high-quality building materials. Patent differences also existed between Christian cities and Islamic-influenced cities in Europe. The latter were better equipped with public services, which included baths and Koranic schools. Finally, in contrast to preceding centuries, the Romanesque era had to find structures with well-defined technical functions designated to a new social category, the traveller: a mixed sub-culture of pilgrims, musicians, artists, merchants, mercenaries, artisans and monks all sharing the same objective of being able to use roads that were comfortable and secure. The improvement of transport on wheels and the increased safety of the countryside (where larger and larger areas were being used for agricultural purposes and reclaimed from woods and swamps) led to an incremental rise in traffic around and between medieval cities. All this then inspired prestigious civic works, such as city walls, gates, roads, bridges, mills, canals, inns, hospitals and kilns.

The Romanesque house

When discussing the typical Romanesque home today, we refer typically to stone structures from the 11th and 12th centuries, in a number of European locations. They are largely isolated instances, as opposed to large-scale residential complexes, and have survived despite a profoundly altered urban fabric. Surviving examples of homes from this era provide us with a precise idea of living practices around Europe during the first centuries of the second millennium. The chief examples are in Saint-Gilles in Provence and Cluny in Burgundy, France; Trier, Koblenz, Karden and Boppard in the German regions of the southern Rhine; Tournai on the River Scheldt and Ghent on the River Leie, in Belgium; and, one of the best examples, Ascoli Piceno, in Italy. One of the common characteristics of Romanesque residential buildings is the absence of sculptural decoration on their façades: only the shape and location of the fenestration is made to stand out clearly.

Valentré Bridge, Cahors, France, 1306–1355

At the end of 11th century, Roman bridges had become insufficient in number and quality to handle the increase in traffic in the countryside and around cities. Starting in the mid-12th century, they were replaced by new stone structures that were architecturally bolder. Among them is the fortified bridge at Cahors. With its massive stone pillars and lofty towers, it ranks among the most prestigious works of the period.

Wherever possible, Romanesque homes made use of existing Roman foundations or structures, often consisting of basements or cellars that could be used for storage. The attics were also used to preserve foodstuffs or as granaries. While homes with pitched roofs (to facilitate the flow of snow and rain) were typical of northern areas like the Rhineland or Flanders, and often featured graded façades, in Italy and other southerly regions, the residential façades were embellished with horizontal eaves. One peculiar type of Romanesque habitation was the tower house, of which very few examples remain because they were harvested for materials or demolished over the centuries, mainly for safety reasons. The oldest example is probably the Frankenturm (Tower of the Franks) in Trier, and there are also important examples in Italy, especially in the centre of the country and in the north at Pavia, Albenga, Savona, Alba, Perugia and other places. The most evocative example of the effect they had on the landscape of a medieval town can be seen in San Gimignano, where a number of these structures have been very well preserved. Such towers, which typically belonged to the aristocracy, were built increasingly taller as a result of a somewhat peculiar competition between rival families; they are even out of proportion with the bell towers of the churches or the towers placed next to public buildings. The extremely tall towers of Bologna, for example, were so impressive that even Dante felt compelled to comment on them in his *Divine Comedy*. The one belonging to the Asinelli family comes close to 100 metres (330 feet) in height and has become the symbol of the city.

above left
House in Glastonbury, UK

Glastonbury is the birthplace of Christianity on the British Isles and the site of the first church built to hold the Holy Grail. The town owes its position as a pilgrimage destination to the legend of the landing of Joseph of Arimathea, the guardian of Christ's tomb. Arriving by ship, Joseph set foot on the marshy ground at a point where his staff miraculously bloomed into the so-called Glastonbury Hawthorn (Holy Thorn), a hybrid that grows only here and blooms twice a year.

above right
Palace of the King of Navarre, Estella, Spain, circa 1200

The rectangular building comprises four large semi-circular arches, which lead to a hall on the ground floor, and an upper floor with windows; the second floor and the tower are later additions.

opposite page, bottom
View of San Gimignano, Siena

Founded in the 10th century on the Via Francigena, this village stands out in the Siena countryside not only for the integrity of its structures but also its distinctive group of towers.

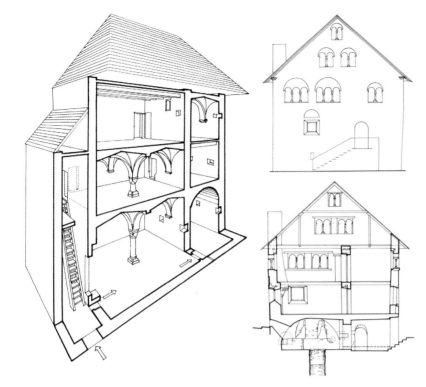

Elevation and sections of a Romanesque house

With the exception of a few later examples, a typical Romanesque house is a rather low building – a maximum of three floors above ground – very simple in plan with two or three interconnected living areas, that is, without corridors. The so-called simple apartment was common to castles until the modern age. The façades of private residences mimic those of palaces with their large entrances on the ground floor and light-filled windows. The interior arrangement is primarily functional, with cellars on a square plan, occasionally supported by pillars, an open ground floor, sometimes used as a warehouse or workshop, a first floor and sometimes a second floor, intended for social and private life, with walls adorned by murals or tapestries.

THE EARLY ROMANESQUE

The early Romanesque style concentrated primarily on the elaboration of two specific building types: imperial cathedrals and Benedictine abbeys. In neither case are we dealing with genuine "novelties", but typologies that had been devloped in previous centuries and, at the dawn of the new millennium, were subjected to some profound reconsideration and reinterpretation, wherein the facets of architecture came to form the basis and the medium for overall aesthetic creativity. For the time being, decorative art production was directly related to buildings: sculpted portals, ornate capitals, slabs with bas reliefs and, on the interior, fresco cycles and other paintings produced in tune with the structural features of the existing church. Indeed, during the stylistic and cultural shift that led to the Romanesque, religious architecture assumed a central role, and not just as an expression of religious devotion in a place of worship. In its highest forms of expression, the architecture of the early Romanesque reflected and interpreted the duality of power between the Holy Roman Empire, based primarily in central Europe, but delegating responsibility for local government to vassals and dukes, and the ecclesiastical hierarchy, headed by the Pope in Rome and spreading its authority to the dioceses through the bishops and to the monastic estates through the abbots.

**Monastery of San Pedro de Roda,
Girona, Spain, consecrated in 1022**

In the absence of proper borders between countries, Europe in the 11th century was highly receptive to cultural exchange and aesthetic mélanges. One of the cohesive elements, however, was the idea of a vast unified empire, relaunched in the 9th century by the Carolingian dynasty, an idea strongly nurtured at the highest levels of culture. Although spread out across Europe, the 11th-century aristocracy was united by the same faith, the same rites, the same language and the same cultural heritage. Above all, it was united by the memory of Charlemagne and of the concept of a "holy Roman" empire, by the prestige of Rome as the capital of the faith and the idea of a secular central power. Imperial cathedrals were originally inspired by the noble example of the Palatine Chapel, founded by Charlemagne at the beginning of the 9th century. But on German soil, they evolved from an octagonal plan to a more linear plan, with an elongated central body formed by a nave and two aisles, terminating in two symmetrically opposite, elaborated eastern and western ends.

The spiritual movement of monasticism became the basis of western European culture; it preserved ancient texts and devised new artistic models. Its promoter, St Benedict of Nursia, had written the *Rule of St Benedict*, which dictated alternate periods of prayer and work, both manual and intellectual. Great Benedictine abbeys were built based on the example

Representation of the Cluniac abbot William of Volpiano, detail of the pulpit in the Basilica of San Giulio, Island of San Giulio, Novara, Italy

William of Volpiano (962–1031) was native to an island on Lake Orta and one of the first great promoters of Romanesque architecture. Very early on, he built the famous rotunda of the ancient Abbey of Saint-Bénigne in Dijon. Later, under the auspices of the Duke of Normandy, he strongly supported building activity in that region, forming a foundation for the development of Norman Romanesque architecture. This legendary figure is commemorated in the pulpit of the Basilica of San Giulio. Although he was a strict and severe monk who imposed a rigorous asceticism on his brother monks, the artist depicted him in the garments of a knight.

of Monte Cassino, founded by the saint back in 529. They proliferated and were adapted to meet the practical, spiritual and material needs of life in monastic communities; they also aimed to protect their economically advantageous positions. Romanesque architecture, with its solidity, its solemnity and its mystical overtones, had its most important expression in Benedictine abbey churches. Still, in the style and distribution of their buildings, Benedictine monasteries did not follow a homogeneous pattern. Quite the opposite was true of the 12th-century abbeys founded by the nascent Cistercian Order, whose architectural features were established and implemented in a more consistent way, according to the austere aesthetics of Saint Bernard of Clairvaux in France.

Continuation and rebirth of the Empire

Religious architecture commissioned by the Holy Roman Empire during the early Romanesque period still considered the church, not the sovereign's royal palace or castle, as the true seat of power. In order to underline the connections with classical antiquity, Charlemagne had wished the Palatine Chapel in Aachen (Aix-la-Chapelle) to be modelled on the churches built in the period from the 4th and 5th centuries. The Basilica of San Lorenzo, connected to the imperial palace in Milan, provided the model for a large central space that was adopted and developed during the subsequent relocations of the imperial capital in the churches of San Vitale in Ravenna and Hagia Sophia in Constantinople. Their octagonal form is reminiscent of a crown, the emblem of the sovereign, and symbolises the mission of the earthly king as intercessor for his people with God by combining the square, symbol of the earth, with the circle, symbol of heaven. The octagon, through which the link is established, becomes a symbol of eternity, according to the numerlogy of the era. The presence of an upper loggia (where the emperor's marble throne was located) raised the figure of the sovereign above the community of his subjects. In addition, in order to visually reinforce the strong links to classical antiquity and early Christianity, Charlemagne commissioned a solemn bronze door along perfect Classical lines for the Palatine Chapel. He also imported "remains" or "fragments" from Rome and Ravenna and entrusted the construction to Lombardian master builders and the famous Comacine masters.

The character of, and developments within, Carolingian architecture were thus directly linked to imperial power and to the Palatine School, organised by historian Eginardo as a true and authentic centre of culture, a centre aware of its own historical role, with a clear intention of merging Roman cultural, aesthetic and technical traditions with Christian spirituality and civilisation. Ecclesiastical teachings and Christian philosophical leanings that were derived from the teachings of St Augustine, closely connected monarchic institutions with revived forms of Roman antiquity. At this time, reforms in the Frankish church were aimed at renewing Christian liturgy and the instruction of clergymen who were entrusted with important duties at the heart of court institutions and monasteries. These duties included the amendment and collection of remnants from the Latin tradition, and the study, transcription and diffusion of the works of church forefathers and classical authors. Their efforts resulted in a major legacy of European culture in subsequent centuries.

West chancel of the Essen Abbey, Essen, Germany, 9th century

The octagon of the abbey church in Essen is an example of Carolingian motifs revived in the Romanesque period. The double arcades with transenna (stone window screens) are clearly derived from the Palatine Chapel at Aachen (Aix-la-Chapelle). The project was commissioned by the energetic abbess, Theophano (997–1058), to accentuate the high rank of the nuns, who were frequently members of the imperial family.

TERRITORIES OF THE HOLY ROMAN EMPIRE

In the 11th century, the pomp and splendour of the Empire were manifested in an artistic flourishing expressed, above all, in religious buildings and their furnishings. A revival of building activity presented itself as a natural development of Carolingian art and, thanks to renewed contacts with Byzantine culture, inspired a renewed verve for spiritual values.

The Romanesque *Westbau*, a turreted complex that completed the western end of church structures, was an architectural motif typical of churches in Germanic Europe. It eliminated the need for a façade and was a direct evolution of the westwork, a multi-storey, structurally functional entryway flanked by towers typical of 9th/10th-century Carolingian and Ottonian architecture. The westwork provided a monumental entrance, while the *Westbau* was less intricate. With the entrance now on the sides of the structure, the westwork is opposite the apsidal section formed by the presbytery and choir, accenting the polarity between the clergy at the eastern end and the imperial court at the western end. The development of the two ends of the church, in the east and in the west, thus determined the lack of a privileged perspective axis. The structure was conceived on a rigorously geometric basis, which used a square as an overall compositional model. From a structural point of view, the building employed walls of great thickness and a flat wooden roof, with the weight distributed on regularly alternating supports. In cathedrals from the early German Romanesque period, the introduction of lateral aisles, double transepts, crypts and loggias – without noting the wealth of furnishings – allows the viewer to imagine the magnificence of the liturgical ceremonies that were being carried out inside this noble, solemn and ideologically charged symbol of imperial power.

Church of St Pantaleon, Cologne, Germany, turn of the 11th century

Among the many Romanesque churches in Cologne, St Pantaleon offers a mature solution that can now be called classic. It is characterised by stone galleries, the exterior articulation through shafts, Lombard bands and round arches. The west body consists of a mighty central tower with a porch below a triangular pediment. Distinctive side towers start from a square basis and develop vertically into an octagonal and then circular shape.

Trier Cathedral, Trier, Germany, 1039–1066

The western façade of Trier Cathedral displays a new way of shaping the exterior by combining architectural elements of the German Romanesque. The majestic westwork becomes an important architectural element thanks to the differentiated surfaces created by the protruding shapes of the west apse and the four towers, and to the chiaroscuro effect of the niches and the loggias along the walls.

With the shift of imperial power to the cities along the corridors of the Rhine and the Meuse rivers, the city of Cologne became the main metropolitan point of reference for central Europe. A powerful episcopal seat, commercial hub and prosperous harbour since its founding in Roman times, Cologne quickly became a nexus of artistic innovation. In just one century, the city was endowed with a considerable number of churches of great architectural and artistic value, both within the old city walls and, in 1106, outside them to protect the northern, southern and western outskirts. From St Maria im Kapitol and the Church of the Holy Apostles, to the Church of St Pantaleon and the Benedictine convent dedicated to Maria Laach, each played a decisive role in the evolution of local Romanesque architecture. Ultimately, this "Rhenish" school of architecture developed a series of styles that made Cologne a highly original spawning ground for European architecture during the 10th, 11th and 12th centuries.

This effective cultural supremacy was confirmed in subsequent centuries by the presence of two great protagonists of religious debate, Alberto Magno (1206–1280) and Duns Scoto (1266–1308), as well as by the construction of the stunning Gothic Cathedral of Great St Martin. This and the other churches in Cologne were badly damaged during World War Two, but have since been rebuilt due to a programme of restoration.

Ground plan and elevation of the chancel of St Maria im Kapitol, Cologne, Germany, 1040–1065

The typical basilica layout in imperial religious buildings did not preclude experimentation with different solutions, especially since Rhenish culture was often inspired by architectural designs of Classical buildings from the ancient Roman Empire, in particular spas and palaces. In the church of St Maria im Kapitol, linked to a rich convent of nuns, the body of the basilica was built between 1040 and 1049, while the chancel with three apses (trefoil) was erected between 1060 and 1065. This represents a fortuitous solution to the architectural challenge of grafting a centrally planned body onto a longitudinal body. The trefoil of three apses is reminiscent of the cella trichora (the three-apse hall of the presbytery) found in many early Christian buildings, and is adopted in order to highlight the Christian and imperial roots of German art. The church, one of the Romanesque masterpieces in the Rhine Valley, bears a name that recalls the ancient presence of a Roman temple on top of a low hill not far from the river, on the outskirts of the ancient Colonia Augusta. The plan below clearly shows the spatial continuity between the basilica body of the three aisles (1) and the centric body of the large exedrae (ample semicircular niches) with ambulatory (2), extended due to the monastic use of the church; it creates a consistency obtained by not differentiating the chancel (3) from the two side exedrae, which here act as a transept.

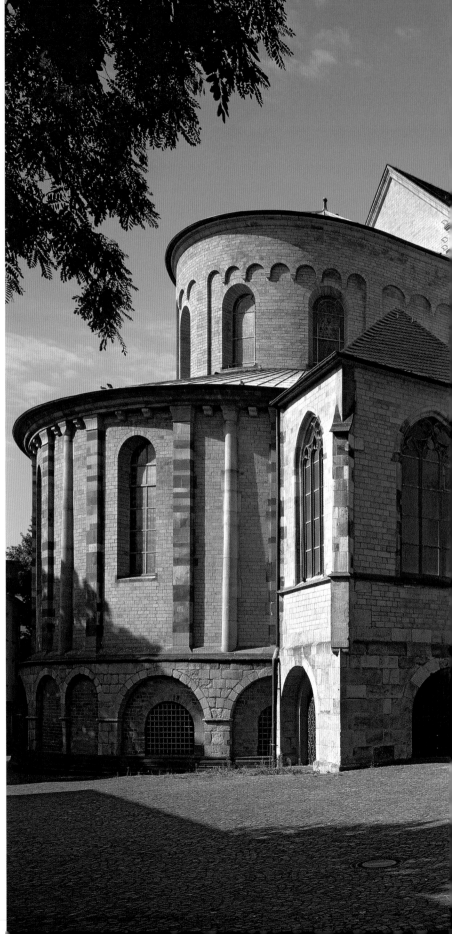

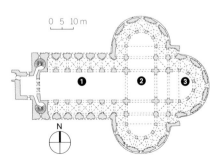

0 5 10 m

N

THE MASTERPIECE
SPEYER CATHEDRAL

Speyer Cathedral was a clear symbol of the power of the Holy Roman Empire in Germany, and the location for official international meetings known as diets. The building was repeatedly enlarged until it was given its present appearance at the end of the 11th century. The reconstruction of the transept and the apse, ordered by Emperor Henry IV after 1095, and the renewal of the central nave in order to enable the addition of the vault, signal the moment when imperial culture fully adhered to the structural and figurative concept of the western Romanesque. The building confirms the tendency of German Romanesque to place great importance on façades by combining solutions typical of the Carolingian and Ottonian tradition (massive volumes enclosed by towers) with elements of Lombard origin, such as shafts, arcades, so-called Lombard bands, galleries and loggias. The façade was rebuilt in the neo-Romanesque style around 1820.

Drawing reconstructing the central nave of Speyer Cathedral, consecrated in 1060 (below left), and its present appearance (below), Germany

Speyer Cathedral has a basilica plan with three naves and a transept. The huge central nave was covered with a stone vault around 1100. The drawing shows a reconstruction of the original flat, wooden ceiling (1). Pilasters with columns (2) support the big blind arches (3), which frame the arcades and the windows.

**below and below right
View and plan of the crypt of
Speyer Cathedral, Germany,
circa 1040**

In the Romanesque period, crypts
took on the look of vast chapels, or
even of a real underground second
church with naves. Their structures
were fully developed by the beginning
of the 11th century; to provide height,
the presbytery had to be raised,
which in turn led to modifications
to the optical effects of the interior
of the church. The ideal shape is the
crypt at Speyer, intended for the
burial of German royalty: it is a
hall with cross vaults lowered onto
isolated columns, and pilasters with
columns, and it fits into the space
of the church above by occupying
the whole extent of the chancel and
transept. The bays are enclosed by
powerful transversal and longitudinal
arches, a typical form of partition in
the early Romanesque.

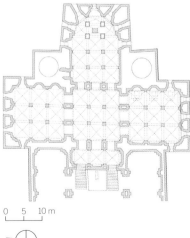

NORTHERN ITALY

At the dawn of the Romanesque era, religious architecture in northern Italy followed late-Classical and early-Byzantine examples; the mid-11th century in Catalonia, Aquitaine and Burgundy saw the first churches completely vaulted in stone; and in Lombardy, architects remained true to the tradition of roofed basilicas, a trend that would continue until the very end of the 11th century. The typical external elements of churches north of the Alps – i.e. the west-work and the towers above the two ends of the transept and the crossing – were uncommon in Italian churches, which favoured a simple exterior that emphasised the interior layout of the building. There were, however, isolated examples of towers that flanked the apse (Ivrea Cathedral from 1002, and the church of Sant'Abbondio in Como), or were inserted into the façade, such as Santa Maria del Tiglio (St Mary of the Lime Tree) at Gravedona. At the same time, as part of a process of assimilation that has always existed between regions north and south of the Alps, churches in the Padana region began adopting some of the motifs and typologies used in the north, such as the apse with ambulatory (walking space) and a western transept. Still, in the Padana region, which included all of northern Italy, with the exception of Venice, Lombard master builders elaborated and expanded on several elements that epitomised the architectural language of the Romanesque. Among those that stood out: the technique of constructing walls with stones of uniform height ("isodomic" stones) cut with even faces and square edges, and that of using flat ribs to reinforce groin vaults, thus defining their distinct surfaces and improving structural integrity.

Santa Maria del Tiglio (St Mary of the Lime Tree), Gravedona, Como, Italy, 12th century

A historical centre of the Alto Lario (northern area around Lake Como, also called Lake Lario), Gravedona is located on the ancient Via Regina, which connects the Po Valley with Coire in the Swiss Canton of Grisons, passing Chiavenna and Splügen on the way. Along this important medieval route, there are numerous Romanesque buildings, often the work of the Comacine masters. The church at Gravedona has a distinctive tall tower with a square base and an octagonal top that juts out at the front.

Santa Maria Maggiore, Lomello, Pavia, Italy, circa 1025

The parish church in Lomello, in the province of Pavia, was built on a previous Lombardian building. Its reconstruction in the beginning of the 11th century anticipates technical solutions that would be adopted later for much larger churches. The central nave, aside from its wooden ceiling, is supported by transversal arches that drop onto pilasters; they not only reinforce the walls but also establish a subtle division into bays in an obvious attempt to subdivide the internal spaces. The introduction of transversal arches to support the roof preceded the building of vaults over the main nave, and is the first element of these future vaults: a solution that architect Lanfranco would adopt in Modena Cathedral at the end of the 11th century.

FRANCE AND CATALONIA

During the 11th century, Normandy developed into an important "laboratory" of architectural experimentation, where architects tried new structural techniques that would not only become clear precursors to several solutions used during the later Gothic period, but which also influenced contemporary British architecture. This innovation, or "renewal", is well represented by the ruins of the church at Bernay Abbey in Normandy (second decade of the 11th century), where the so-called mur épais, or "Norman gallery", was elaborated for the first time – a sort of corridor built in the thick walls at the top of the external fenestration. Many other buildings here, though in ruins now, illustrate fundamental themes that influenced later movements in architecture: the two-tower façade at Jumièges, the "matronea" (women's

opposite page
Abbey Church of Notre-Dame, Jumièges, France, 1040–1067

Though rebuilt in the 11th century, when William of Volpiano was active in Normandy, the only remains of the Abbey Church of Notre-Dame are the nave and the façade, with its two characteristic towers – square bases and octagonal upper sections. The towers enclose the protruding westwork, formed by a vaulted atrium with a tribune above it that is accessed from the tower stairs. Façades flanked by two towers would become a popular design in the 12th century that frequently featured in Gothic cathedrals.

Church of Sant Vicenç, Cardona, Spain, 1029–1040

One of the main innovations of the early Romanesque can be seen in Catalonia, where walls, which were typically built of rubble (or pebbles from a river) bound with mortar, were now being constructed using small, cut stones to ensure their stability. Sant Vicenç brings together all the typical elements of the early Romanesque in southern Europe, combining technical and formal maturity and offering an archetypal example of the spread of Lombard Romanesque in the territories that had been liberated from Moorish control. The exterior walls are enlivened by blind arcades, while the interior features a rather bare, austere and compact structure. A prominent dome rises on the crossing and is masked on the outside by an octagonal tiburium (a polygonal structure that hides the dome). This constitutes the pivot around which the volumes of the apse and transept are organised.

galleries) in the longitudinal naves at the Bayeaux and Coutances cathedrals, the tripartite choir and blind triforium at Bernay, and the aisled crypt and ambulatory choir of the cathedral in Rouen. Meanwhile, at the Basilica of St Martin in Tours, France, we see for the first time the outline of an ambulatory choir with radiating chapels, a solution that saw its greatest expression in churches constructed later, along pilgrimage routes at the end of the 11th and 12th centuries.

Conversely, the neighbouring territories of the French crown, the so-called Domaine Royale, including Ile-de-France, Champagne and Picardy, remained fundamentally faithful to imperial Salian culture throughout the 11th century. It was a borderland with a predominance of proto-Romanesque basilicas featuring flat ceilings surmounted by towers and a marked articulation of the walls. Saint-Étienne at Vignory, Saint-Remi at Reims and Saint-Germain des Prés, the oldest church still standing in Paris, are examples of this style. The territories between the Loire in France and the Douro in Spain also offer a specialised and original spectrum of buildings within the panorama of early-Romanesque architecture. Between the 10th and the 11th

Plan, transversal section of the chancel and isometric perspective of Saint-Étienne, Vignory, France

This church possesses a basilica plan with one central nave and two aisles strengthened near the crossing, (1) to support a tower – in this case, one that was never built. The chancel (2) has an ambulatory (3) built on pilasters alternating with columns (4) with radial chapels (5). A tower rises above one side aisle north of the apse (6).

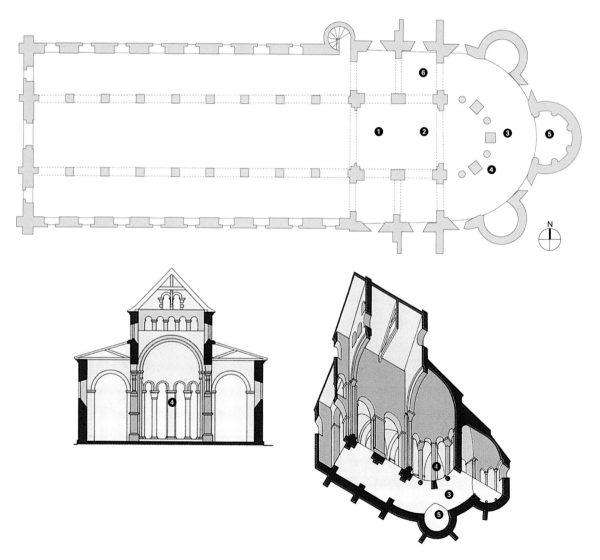

centuries, Catalonia in particular witnessed an extraordinary proliferation of churches built on a new model that would be of fundamental importance in the future of European architecture: the hall church, with nave and aisles of equal height, usually with a barrel vault of semicylindrical appearance. Deriving from the Carolingian westwork concept, and including the aisled crypts (which presupposed flat flooring above), it became a very original space when it formed the main interior of a church. They were solid, fire-proof constructions made entirely of stone, with thick, compact walls and rather dark interiors – no windows in the nave, so-called blind naves – where only dim light filtered in from the aisles and the apse. There was a total absence of sculptural decoration inside, and on the outside, the surfaces were framed by pilasters and arches that created a dynamic and pictorial effect. Although Burgundy showed significant originality and innovation in the 11th century, the styles there were most certainly influenced by proto-Romanesque Catalan architecture. Indeed, the dominant building type here was the hall church. However, another typical form of medieval architecture also developed in the region that would spread widely in southern France and northern Spain starting at the end of the 11th century. It would feature the following: a church with one nave, covered with a barrel vault or a dome.

Nave of the Church of Saint-Étienne, Vignory, France, consecrated in 1050

The introduction of new concepts of spatial relations in the Church of Saint-Étienne earned the building an important place in architectural history, and in the evolution of churches with ambulatories. The nave with wooden ceiling has vertical openings in the shape of a false matroneum. This opens onto the side aisles and has columns with capitals sculpted in stylised geometrical and plant motifs: a rare solution derived from antiquity that announces the rebirth of monumental sculpture.

THE MASTERPIECE
THE ABBEY CHURCH OF ST PHILIBERT IN TOURNUS

The long main body of the Abbey Church of St Philibert (1008–1056) is one of the most surprising achievements of the early Romanesque in Burgundy. In both its wall decoration and its architectural structure, the church testifies to the arrival of more southerly influences in the region. In front of the church, there is an imposing narthex (1) with three vaulted bays (a covered atrium set on columns or pilasters, still influenced by the Carolingian two-storey westwork concept). Inside are three naves (2) with imposing circular pilasters (3) in cut stone; these enable the unusual height of the side aisles and almost give it the look of a hall church. The clerestory (4) has windows directly illuminating the central nave, the chancel has an ambulatory (5) and three rectangular radial chapels (6), and below the church is a large crypt (7).

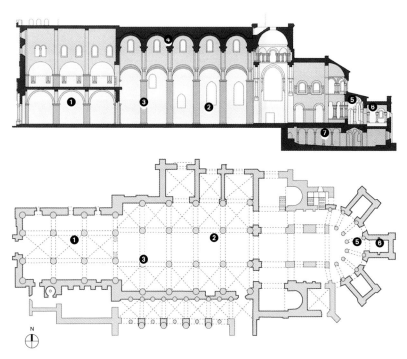

Section and plan of St Philibert, Tournus, France

right
Vaulted central nave of St Philibert, Tournus, France

In the middle of the 11th century, the original wooden roof here was replaced by transverse barrel vaults supported by arch-shaped structures, an aesthetically daring yet, from a structural viewpoint, functional solution: the barrel vault allowed for the windows to be enlarged and admit direct sunlight.

THE LATER ROMANESQUE

The almost universal adoption of the barrel-vaulted ceiling was a symbol, not only of contemporary advances in construction techniques, but also of conscious stylistic choices that enabled the development of innovative systems of structural support and roofing. Such solutions were, in turn, integrated into different methods of articulation for walls, which were marked by a pattern of bays and a horizontal division in tiers not only in the nave, but also extending to the rest of the church, including the exterior. This redesign was based on the intention of welcoming and accommodating the faithful, while still surrounding them with a space that was both solemn and severe; it was to be characterised by strong tonal effects and employ contrasts of light and dark in order to stretch the perspective and depth of the interior, all culminating in the glorious apse. The most sacred areas of these churches were separated by rails and reserved for members of the clergy, but buildings of larger dimensions were often endowed with an ambulatory: a wide corridor that ran behind the presbytery and the choir (following the curve of the apse itself), and accessible to all worshippers. The ambulatory was an ideal space for increasingly common ritual processions as well as for accommodating additional altars and areas for the adoration of holy relics.

Central nave of the abbey church in Lessay, Normandy, France, late 11th century

From a structural point of view, the architecture of the late Romanesque differed from earlier periods in its adoption of a system of bays, spatial cells ordered in a rigidly symmetrical fashion. The isolated crossing, a zone produced by the confluence of the nave and the transept, then became the norm, and the central point of the building, providing the rest with order and proportion. At the same time, the walls underwent a distinct transformation: they could now be segmented, hollowed out and sometimes even used to create an internal corridor. The replacement of the column with pilasters became almost universal, with the exception of Italy, where architectural decoration and monumental sculpture became more common – though it never eclipsed the architectural function. Beyond these churches, the advent of civic society produced important innovations in urban design and architecture. The assertion of this new urban autonomy was particularly reflected in the organisation of city squares, where space was often defined by the arrangement of various buildings (churches, bell towers, baptisteries and palaces) and used for the key activities of both secular and religious life. City halls, which were often accessed via loggias and porticoes, became the key symbols of the civic pride, independence and economic wealth of these growing municipalities.

below
Parma Cathedral, Italy,
11th–12th century,

This cathedral overlooks an urban landscape that is a model for coherent layout and homogeneous style. The façade shows various orders of loggias: a sculptural effect underlined by light and shade, and the colourful effect of the materials. On the side are the bell tower and the isolated late-Romanesque baptistery.

opposite page
Ambulatory of the Abbey
of Sant'Antimo, Siena, Italy,
12th century

Located along the ancient Via Francigena, Sant'Antimo features a wide ambulatory in the French style, running around the chancel.

Great lords and courtly life in the feudal era

The medieval world did not comprise "nations" in the modern sense. During the 11th and 12th centuries, a broad swathe of central Europe consisted of small and large territories coexisting within the political context of the Holy Roman Empire, which struggled to maintain unity and order – a task it never fully achieved. Indeed, many communities continually sought to better define their respective identities.

Until the beginning of the 11th century, society itself was a reflection of the Kingdom of God, with the emperor at the head of the worldly realm. Arthur, Charlemagne, Alexander the Great, King David and other chivalric heroes were king figures, and the permanence of the myth of the monarch is one of the characteristics of medieval civilisation. But the establishment of a feudalistic society brought changes with it. In more highly evolved countries, especially France, for example, new social structures emerged, bringing with them repercussions for all levels of secular society – mostly regarding the distribution of wealth and power. The decadence of monarchic rule, despite its endurance in popular consciousness and mythical representations, resulted in the gradual breakdown of the state, allowing favour, authority and, ultimately, power to shift to local squires, who became undisputed overlords ruling despotically in the territories under their control. These feudal lords came to regard the powers devolved to them as their own personal power, exercising them freely and passing them down through their sons.

During the 11th century, new kings were anointed and crowned (despite established kingdoms) and no one doubted these authorities; military power and legal rights to judge and punish were nonetheless scattered among a system of political "cells". The "squire" was typically a member of some

below
Detail of the *Bayeaux Tapestry*, Centre Guillaume-le-Conquérant, Bayeux, France, circa 1066–1082

Woven in Canterbury, this famous tapestry was commissioned by Odo, Bishop of Bayeux, with the aim of displaying it in the town cathedral. The narrative technique recalls epic literary tradition, and the scenes are set within areas limited by stylised ornamental motifs, accompanied by didactic inscriptions. The embroidery recounts the Norman conquest of England and celebrates William the Conqueror, creator of the model feudal state. It is also a matchless depiction of daily life in the 11th century: the first part illustrates scenes from court life, such as falcon hunting and banquets.

dynasty, firmly based on his geographical territory. Like the king, he believed himself ordained to maintain peace and justice in the name of God. The intricate web of rights that allowed him to exercise this duty was traced back to his castle. The tower, primarily a symbol of a sovereign entity, and secondly of regal power in its military capacity, became the centre of personal power and the foundation of the prestige and authority of a dynasty. The distribution of political power and all the structures of the new society were organised around that. Knights, who enjoyed the privilege of carrying arms, were spared feudal servitude, but repaid their lords by fulfilling obligations they had agreed to through an oath of homage and fealty. This system resulted in a new and smaller royal court that valued the virtues of courage, strength, generosity and loyalty. The castle thus became a fortified home for knights at arms, and thus the seat of administration and jurisdiction, protecting against invasion and controlling the major routes of communication. However, inside its walls, the castle gradually became the setting for a luxurious court culture characterised by banquets, processions and tournaments.

Loarre Castle, Spain, 11th–13th century

This castle overlooks the plain of the River Ebro in northern Aragon, a frontier zone that was subjected to occasional Moorish military forays. The citadel's main area is encircled by a ring of walls and twelve towers dating from the 13th century; it also houses a church, whose unusual size and rich decoration renders uncertain the true function of the complex. The defensive purpose, fending off the Moors, who had taken over much of the Iberian Peninsula, had lost its importance in the years when the complex was actually built, so Loarre was presumably used as a residence by the kings of Aragon and Navarre.

Urban and rural fortresses

Alongside church architecture, castles and fortresses represent the other side of an era in which secular structures, from northern Europe all the way to Sicily, have a lot in common with regard to design. The castle, originally dedicated to defending frontiers and communication routes, ultimately became a central point of reference for vast territories, not only as the seat of administration but also as the residence of the feudal nobility. At the start of the 11th century, the fragmentation of feudal power was reflected in the sheer number of fortified castles built and, in vernacular architecture, the completely new types of buildings that were developed. Designs gradually moved away from the high medieval fortress, instead incorporating new defensive technologies and other elements intended to meet the latest expectations with regard to habitability. In the early years of the Romanesque, fortresses were still constructed from wood and surrounded by a bastion and a ditch. The keep then became the model for castles built of stone, with primarily defensive structures including fortified towers, watchtowers and walls as well as areas designed for living purposes – a sign of social change. The French "donjon" and the Anglo-Norman keep not only met security needs but was also a symbol of power. In England, as in France, primitive keeps evolved from simple rectangular shapes (Canterbury) to circular and octagonal shapes (Conisbrough). Advances in defensive concepts inspired these developments: by eliminating "redundant" corners, fewer surfaces were exposed to the increasing range of available weapons.

Free city-states and Italian fortified cities

Historical events prevented the creation of what one could refer to as a "typical" structure in Italy, unlike in the rest of western Europe. Instead of a building style, autonomous, fortified cities emerged there, characterised by a variety of social, economic and political elements, with a correspondingly diverse range of solutions and architectural forms. From the market towns of Moorish Sicily to the free city-states of central-northern Italy, and from the maritime republics to the hill towns in the Apennine region, it is not easy to identify precise urban typologies and lines of development. Though the Normans impeded the development of cities in the south with their feudal structure and dominant elite class, the maritime cities of Amalfi, Venice, Pisa and Genoa flourished in an era of great splendour along with the port cities of Bari and Brindisi, where arriving and departing ships connected Europe to the Holy Land. By contrast, central-northern Italy's predilection for polycentrism and self-government was based on two different dynamics: the Apennine region's pronounced need for defence, which led to a proliferation of small fortified settlements, and the Padana region's strength in the area of communications, which led to economic and social growth that put cities in a dominant position, with a hegemony over the territories surrounding them. The unique and magnificent exception to this was Venice, the only city without direct Roman origins and one that continued to develop, occupying the islands of the Venetian lagoon and adapting its urban structure according to its specific natural topography.

Crusaders and chivalric orders

The Crusades represent one of the most controversial chapters in the history of the Roman Catholic Church. They not only focused on the reconquest of

The keep at Conisbrough, UK, 12th century

In the 12th century, English keeps became more and more complex in their design. At Conisbrough, the circular central tower is flanked by smaller, rectangular towers set diagonally and grafted on at regular intervals.

**opposite page
White Tower, London, UK, 1078**

To maintain their claim to power over newly conquered territory, the Normans erected fortified buildings all over southern England. The White Tower defended London on the banks of the Thames: it is a square-plan structure with four small towers at the corners. It is a prime example of the multiple functions of the Anglo-Norman keep, at once a fortress, a royal palace, a prison and the seat of government. It was the centre of the English monarchy and the symbol of the reign of William the Conqueror (1066–1087).

the Holy Land, but were also viewed by crusaders as an opportunity for personal salvation. The Church, which up until this point had sought to defend
itself from violence between rival kingdoms, felt compelled to call upon
the chivalric orders for assistance, thus channelling their warring activities
into a misleadingly named "pacifist movement for God", all based on an
interpretation of feudalism that fit into prevailing Christian attitudes. A new
tradition was born of holding initiation ceremonies on the day of Pentecost
so warriors would be enlightened by the power of the Holy Spirit.

The words of the initiation blessed the crusaders' swords, assigned the
armed believers with the mission of war against the "infidel" and motivated
them to pursue the "noble" goal of liberating Christ's Holy Sepulchre
through violence. The cross thus took on a new significance. Until then, it had
remained one of the many symbols that helped bring awareness of the
power of God in the world – a cosmic sign, an axis of space and time, a tree
of life and an emblem of peace. But now it was embroidered on robes worn
by crusaders, marking them with the emblem of their paschal sacrifice.
The crusading orders were also unique in their focus on holy war and
their inclusion of a vow of poverty, chastity and obedience. They were subject
to ecclesiastical law, thus becoming the foundation of a standing army for
Catholic states in the Near East and for the Iberian kingdoms, with sizeable

forts built in strategic points and controlling those territories. During the First Crusade, from 1097 to 1099, French crusaders led by Godfrey of Bouillon conquered the Holy Land, which remained under their control for nearly two centuries. From this point onwards, Palestine and the neighbouring territories became an architectural domain of southern France, almost totally devoid of Islamic influence. At the time, religious sculpture was represented as symbols of divine power in coats of arms, armour, helmets, shields and a whole plethora of "weapons" against the powers of evil.

Pilgrimage routes

The reasons for and methods of the spread of Romanesque architecture can be found in the mobility, frequency and multiplicity of relationships in the medieval world. These exchanges happened either along maritime routes or along trade routes connecting urban, mercantile centres and the great religious sanctuaries. The movement of goods and people was derived not only from an economic revival and military campaigns, but also from the custom of going on pilgrimages along routes that led to Rome, Puglia, the Holy Land or to the tomb of the apostle St James in Santiago de Compostela. There, along the beaches of the Atlantic, the "shells of St James" were placed on the coats and hats of pilgrims and soon became the symbol of all pilgrims travelling through Europe.

During this period, guides for pilgrims became more common. The *Codex Calixtinus* (circa 1139), also known as *The Book of St James*, provided advice

The Krak des Chevaliers, Homs, Syria, middle of the 12th century

The Krak des Chevaliers is the most important fortified military structure of the Knights Hospitallers. Built on the foundations of a previous Kurdish castle, halfway between Aleppo and Damascus, it held a strategic position (at the time) on the only pass linking the Mediterranean coast to the hinterland.

opposite page
Dome of the Church of the Holy Sepulchre, Torres del Río, Spain, 12th/13th century

Located on the pilgrimage route that crosses Navarre and leads to Santiago de Compostela in Galicia, the church at Torres del Río has a simple octagonal plan without a central chapel. The dome looks like a starred vault with flat interwoven ribs of Moorish origin, emphasised by the light entering from thin slits at the base of the ribs.

to pilgrims, including itineraries, sermons and liturgical texts. A pilgrimage in medieval times was not just seen as an act of penance and expiation, but also as an effective method of securing divine protection. It was not merely a physical path, but also a spiritual one; indeed, it was the best and most widely accepted form of asceticism available to faithful Christians in the 11th and 12th centuries. Penitence was an instrument of purification imposed by a bishop, but it was also a symbol of the chosen people making their way to the promised land. Apart from the three main destinations (Jerusalem, Rome and Santiago) for the veneration of Jesus and the tombs of the apostles Peter, Paul and James, pilgrims also headed for the apparition sites at the Chapel of Saint Michel d'Aiguilhe in Le Puy-en-Velay, Mont-Saint-Michel in Normandy and the Sacra di San Michele in the Susa Valley.

Over the course of the 11th century, pilgrimages grew increasingly popular, aided by better security on the roads, sanctuaries along the way where relics were kept, and by hospices and monasteries. As a result, many of the most innovative and grandiose complexes of Romanesque Europe were built along these routes, particularly in the provinces of southern France near locations where miracles had supposedly occurred.

Map of the Via Francigena, with German sanctuaries and the pilgrimage embarkation points for Jerusalem and Santiago de Compostela

(1) Canterbury
(2) Reims
(3) Besançon
(4) Lausanne
(5) Pavia
(6) Fidenza
(7) Parma
(8) Siena
(9) Viterbo
(10) Rome
(11) Basle
(12) Strasbourg
(13) Worms
(14) Bonn
(15) Münster
(16) Bremen
(17) Bari
(18) Brindisi
(19) Saint-Gilles-du-Gard
(20) Roncisvalle

In 990, the Archbishop of Canterbury, Sigerico, described the itinerary that led, in 79 stages and with possible local variations, from his "bishop's see" in England to Rome. The route he took, called both the Via Francigena (through France) or the Via Romea (to Rome), is one of the main pilgrim and merchant routes in medieval central Europe, connecting all the most important Christian locations in the region. The other main destinations were the great German cathedrals along the Rhine, Jerusalem and the sanctuary of Santiago de Compostela, in Galicia, Spain. The latter could be reached via various routes departing from four different French localities (Conques, Vézelay, Tours and Toulouse), all of which joined at the Roncevaux Pass before crossing the Pyrenees.

Exterior and plan of the Basilica of the Holy Sepulchre, Jerusalem, Israel, middle of the 12th century

The Basilica of the Holy Sepulchre, an extremely important destination for medieval pilgrims, still maintains the same look it was given in the 12th century – notwithstanding numerous renovations from the 19th century. It comprises a series of structures built in the Constantinian era that mark the sites of the Passion of Christ. Next to St Helena's crypt is a "hole" that is now the Chapel of the Invention of the Cross. On the site of the crucifixion is the Altar of the Crucifixion, while the Rotunda of Anastasis (Resurrection) is on the site of Christ's burial. The ground plan of the Holy Sepulchre shows a monumental circular apse (1), with three semicircular radial chapels (2) and a matroneum. The Anastasis – a centrally planned structure – crowns a church with a transept (3) and a chancel featuring an ambulatory with radial chapels (4). On the transept crossing is a dome connected by squinches (5).

following page, top
Dome of the Temple Church, London, UK, 1185–1240

Built on the model of the Holy Sepulchre, and consecrated by the Patriarch of Jerusalem, the oldest circular body of this Knights Templar church in London rises on two levels; the wooden dome, on the second level, is inside a hexagonal perimeter. Some details of the rotunda suggest close links with the Orient, such as the tombstones of the knights, where the human figures are cross-legged, a detail in medieval times that identified crusaders who had fought in the Holy Land.

following page, bottom
San Lorenzo, Mantua, Italy, end of the 11th century

Built in approximately 1083, on the orders of Matilda of Canossa, a feudatory of Mantua, this church is articulated in two concentric circular bodies, with a circular area covered by a dome as well as an ambulatory with two orders, or arcades. The scheme recalls both the Holy Sepulchre in Jerusalem and the Palatine Chapel in Aachen, two noble models interpreted in Lombard fashion with the use of brickwork and exterior shafts decorated with Lombard bands.

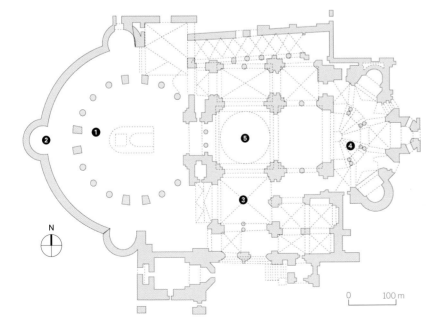

N

0   100 m

The revival of centrally planned churches

The early Christian Church in Rome had built its baptisteries on circular ground plans because the purification rituals that raised man toward God took place there. The choice of centrally planned churches is linked to the funerary tradition of the martyria, or reliquary tombs, as well as to the fact that pilgrims arriving at the Church of the Holy Sepulchre in Jerusalem entered a circular sanctuary, hence the development of this architectural form, which in the 11th century spread throughout Europe and to its easternmost boundaries. In Romanesque architecture, centrally planned buildings almost always took the Palatine Chapel in Aachen or the Church of the Holy Sepulchre at Jerusalem as models. The central plan was reserved for quite specific functions: as a baptistery, particularly in Italy, which could take on monumental dimensions, as in Florence, Cremona, Parma and Pisa; as a chapel in great houses, especially in the territories north of the Alps, as in Kobern in the Rhineland; or as a church, as in the Church of the Holy Sepulchre in Bologna, which largely adopted the ground plan of the archetypal model in Jerusalem.

Different architectural types were often found in specific geographical regions. In Provence and in central-southern Italy, we find the simple octagon without secondary wings, a late-Classical tradition, while circular structures with an ambulatory were relatively rare and almost exclusively limited to northern Italy (at Almenno San Salvatore near Bergamo, Bologna, Mantua and Asti).

The complex of Santo Stefano with the Church of the Holy Sepulchre, Bologna, Italy, 12th century

THE WAY OF ST JAMES

Pilgrimage churches on the Way of St James were situated on mountain roads in the Pyrenees and scattered across the rugged landscape of northern Spain. The cathedral in Santiago de Compostela in Galicia, the destination, is one of the most significant achievements of the Romanesque period, in a class with other churches on the route, including Sainte-Foy Abbey Church in Conques, St Sernin in Toulouse, St-Étienne in Nevers and the Basilica of St Mary Magdalene at Vézelay. They represent significant stages on a path of prayer and penance, but also of cultural and commercial progress. The symbolic value of parts of the cathedral, such as its portals and capitals, was reflected in an extraordinary figurative repertoire that underlined the providential and cosmic order of creation and redemption. The route to Santiago represented a pilgrimage of the soul to God, the stages of which were marked by ancient churches that were rebuilt during the Romanesque.

The Cathedral of Santiago de Compostela was a reflection of a mobile society in northern Spain and southern France that adhered to the international model of pilgrimage churches. The smaller churches located on the mountain passes of the Pyrenees and Galicia, on the other hand, followed local traditions. All the buildings constructed along the Way of St James were funded by monarchs, a demonstration of the interest that the kings of Spain held in such pilgrimages. They were not merely economically motivated, but were also meant to consolidate Christian hegemony in Iberia, which had been reconquered after a long period of Moorish rule.

The apse of Sainte-Foy Abbey, Conques, France, 11th/12th century

Sainte-Foy Abbey in Conques, France, is one of the oldest pilgrimage churches on the Way of St James. The austere exterior is characterised by a vertical and a horizontal articulation, with the chapels radiating from the ambulatory of the chancel and with the apse staggered with the lantern tower on the crossing. Overlapping volumes were characteristic of Romanesque art and created a structure that perfectly suited the need for pilgrims to circulate.

Church of San Martín, Frómista, Spain, circa 1066

The Church of San Martín was commissioned by the widow of the king of Navarre and shows influences of southern, early-Romanesque styles, especially the fairly small exterior walls. With three aisles, the church has a dome on the crossing, masked from outside by an octagonal tower, while the west façade is flanked by two small, cylindrical towers. The repetition of decorative motifs that wrap around the building, from the sculpted cornice under the eaves and the deeply set openings to the semicolumns that extend all the way to the roof, gives the exterior a harmonious appearance.

Panteón de los Reyes, Basilica of Saint Isidore, León, Spain, circa 1063–1100

This collegiate church in León, built to house the relics of Saint Isidore of Seville, was enlarged to the west with a very special space: the so-called Panteón de los Reyes (Royal Pantheon), the royal burial chapel that is now the oldest part of the complex. Structured with bays that are 3 x 3 metres (10 x 10 feet) and supported by pilasters and columns, the chapel is notable not only for the elegant articulation of the walls and the vault, but also for its refined capital sculptures and frescoes, distributed on a white background; their iconographic variety and chromatic richness distinguish them from other works of the time. They depict scenes from the Gospels and the Apocalypse as well as everyday scenes, with seasonal activities, the months of the year and the zodiac all given mention. Lastly, a Christ in Glory is surrounded by the tetramorph (the four evangelists). Elegant inscriptions also accompany and facilitate the interpretation of the images. The Panteón, a royal and dynastic monument, shows how the lords of Castile hoped to achieve salvation by being buried next to their great sovereign. Pilgrims on the way to Santiago de Compostela also prayed for intercession here.

THE MASTERPIECE
THE CATHEDRAL OF SANTIAGO DE COMPOSTELA

The Cathedral of Santiago de Compostela (begun circa 1075) is the final destination of the pilgrimage leading to the tomb of St James. It is the largest Romanesque church in Spain and among the greatest in Europe. Its design is based on the most advanced models of the period: a single-nave basilica with two aisles and "matronea", a transept and a chancel with ambulatory. Following tradition, the sanctuary of Santiago de Compostela was built on the site where Bishop Teodemiro, guided by a star (hence the city's name, "campus stellae"), had found the burial place of St James, an apostle of Jesus chosen as the protector of Christian Spain. The walls are articulated in two storeys, with no windows on the top level of a barrel-vaulted main nave (blind nave). The dim lighting comes from the windows of the side aisles; only the chancel has its own windows, which cast light on the tomb of the saint. The huge dimensions of the church is a direct consequence of the enormous influx of pilgrims. The cruciform plan is articulated in two aisles and a nave preceded by a narthex (1) and leading onto the transept (2), equipped with four small apses (3) on the eastern side; the chancel with ambulatory (4) expands into five radial chapels (5).

Ground plan (right), interior (above) and Pórtico da Gloria (opposite page) of the Cathedral of Santiago de Compostela, Spain, 1075–1122

The statue of the saint, which adorns the trumeau (a dividing central pilaster with stone figures) of the double Pórtico da Gloria by Mateo, welcomes pilgrims and at the same time marks the symbolic access to the destination cathedral; the tympanum depicts themes from the Last Judgement and the Apocalypse.

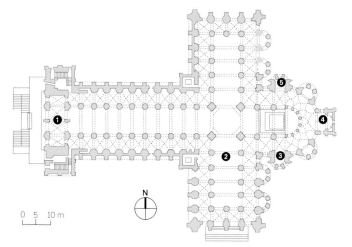

ANGLO-NORMAN ARCHITECTURE

The geographical area in Europe influenced by Norman architecture grew dramatically following the conquest of England in 1066. However, the phenomenon quickly turned into an anomaly. After developing a building designed for a vaulted roof (at Jumièges), the concept was renounced for approximately sixty years while local churches awaited a definitive intervention. The stone vaults of the two great abbeys in Caen (St-Étienne and Le Trinité) were built between 1125 and 1130, but in Britain, the adoption of architectural forms from the continent was already in full swing by 1066. A diversity of developments and solutions can be seen when comparing the roofs above principal naves. The innovative cruciform vault at Durham Cathedral, with its pointed transverse arches, was first attempted in Caen over twenty-five years later but was not widely adopted in the UK thereafter. British master builders continued to build large basilicas with standard roofs. Compared to their French counterparts, churches in the UK were different mainly due to their dimensions, with drastically extended naves and transepts. These cathedrals, traditionally articulated and built on three levels, presented highly structured walls, thanks to the horizontal flights of the arcades and matronea, the presence of the "Norman gallery" in front of the windows (a corridor sunk into the thick walls) and the massive pilasters, which all combined to create a powerful overall effect. The most frequently used motif on the façade was the sizeable central window, which occupied a large part of the space.

opposite page
An arm of the transept of Ely Cathedral, 1090–1130

The nave and transept here show great architectural and artistic quality in the perspective created by the extremely high walls. The sequence includes deeply set arcades, the bipartite openings of the matroneum, the "Norman Gallery" in front of the windows and the pilasters with semicolumns rising to the base of the roof. However, the structure of English cathedrals, like in Franco-Norman churches before 1130, which was apparently suited to masonry vaults, does not reach its utmost potential: their vaults are simply concave with decorative, painted ceilings.

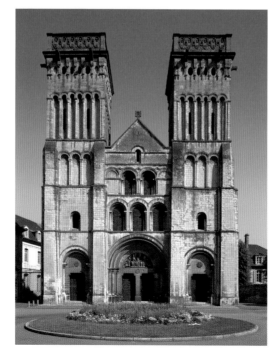

Le Trinité Church, Caen, France, begun 1060–1065

Like its neighbour, St-Étienne (a monastery for men), La Trinité (formerly a cloister for women) represents the purist form of a Romanesque façade, with two towers, abstract cubic volumes and perfect balance with the transversal body. The style would be developed throughout the 12th century and become common in the early-Gothic cathedrals of northern France.

THE MASTERPIECE
DURHAM CATHEDRAL

In the panorama of Norman architecture, the link between French architectural expression and technical tradition and the innovative ability of the English builders is represented best by Durham Cathedral. Vaulted entirely in stone, it is one of the first great constructions of the late Romanesque period, along with Speyer and Cluny III. Durham consists of a huge, elongated body with one nave and two aisles on alternate supports, a matroneum, a wide transept – double and protruding – and a triple chancel. It has the architectural form of a Romanesque building – except for the shape of the vaults – seen in the structural use of thick walls and the powerful mass of cylindrical columns and enormous pilasters. The first large, cross-ribbed

vaults with pointed arches were built in the chancel between 1099 and 1104: a "linguistic" and technical innovation with the aim of lightening and lifting the heavy Romanesque walls, thus foreshadowing forms and characters that would later define Gothic architecture. The choice of the vault at Durham represents the pivotal moment when the problem of giving solidity to the roofing becomes a more general, structural problem of guaranteeing stability for the entire construction. The buttresses hidden beneath the roof coordinate with the matronea and already possess the shape and function of the flying buttresses (arches used to counteract the thrust of the vault) later used to support central vaults.

opposite page
Central nave of Durham Cathedral, UK, 1093–1133

The central nave here balances the solid proportions of the arcades, which are almost 22 meters (72 feet) high in their vaults; it is a unique variant of the segmented vault that would appear later. The arcades have a very distinct rectangular format, and each pilaster has a cruciform section constructed from a band of columns arranged around a round pier. Architectural decoration on a zig-zag, incised, reticulated or spiral form – typical of Norman era decoration – were for the first time incised into the posts of the columns, thus underlining their mass and forming a grandiose and alternating rhythm that gave a solemn dignity to this masterpiece.

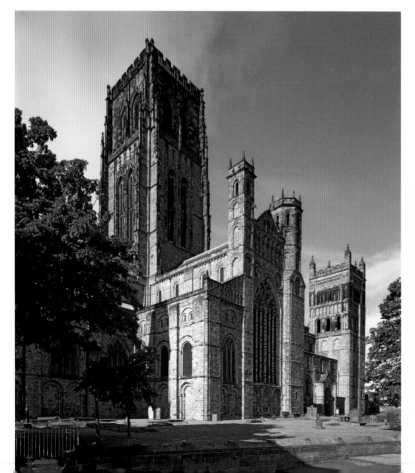

Exterior of Durham Cathedral, UK, 1093–1133

This cathedral, built between 1093 and 1133, has long been an important pilgrim destination in the UK; it houses the relics of St Cuthbert. Together with the monastery and the castle, it is located on a defensible rise above the river Wear. Its lofty location underlines the power and solidity of Norman architecture and the Romanesque spirit in England. The twin-tower façade and the massive square tower on the crossing emphasise the building's impact, while the long northern flank shows the full 143 metres (472 feet) of the nave.

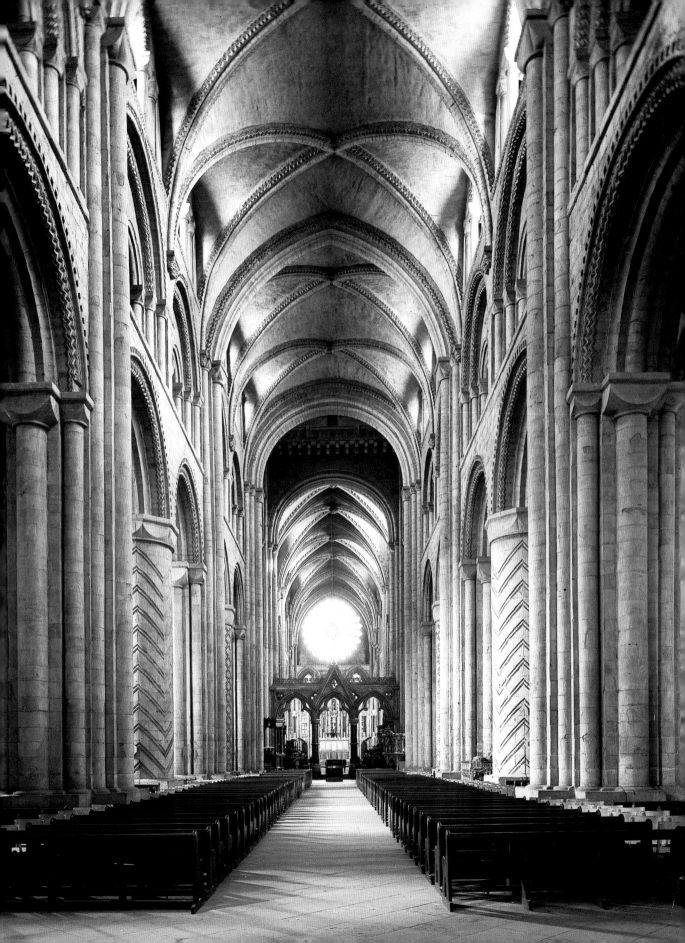

BURGUNDY AND SOUTHERN FRANCE

The Romanesque style manifested itself in Burgundy shortly before the year 1100. It continued there until the middle of the 12th century, with its own regional variation of the vaulted basilica, as seen in the extremely important group of churches called Paray-le-Monial-Cluny III. These churches were based on existing structures with barrel vaults, as in Tournus, and demonstrated the maturation of a local architectural language as well as the gradual simplification of proportions. The barrel vault was given a pointed profile while the windows, once set inside the vault, were now located in the upper portion of the wall, a statement of great beauty and originality. Walls and pilasters were covered by fluted shafts and cornices – as at St Lazare in Autun or Paray-le-Monial – displaying a perfect formal equilibrium unique in Romanesque architecture; it was almost certainly influenced by the Roman ruins in the region. The central nave continued into the transept and the choir, achieving a certain continuity of space that heralded later Gothic cathedrals, but the barrel vault system, with its powerful lateral thrust, prevented the creation of truly spacious naves like those in Lombardy and in the Rhine region. The barrel vaulted churches in Burgundy were thus tall and straight.

View of the domes of Saint-Front Cathedral, Périgueux, France, 1173

Drawing on architectural models used for centuries in the Eastern Roman Empire, single-nave churches in the Aquitaine region were often built on square plans, with four arcades from which a semispherical dome rises. The churches therefore feature a succession of equal domes aligned along a straight axis. Saint-Front is the most famous example of this style.

At the turn of the 11th century, architects in southern France had begun using new construction techniques and building the first completely vaulted basilicas. During the 12th century, this situation continued. The most frequent designs were the single-chamber church, which reflected the characteristics of the proto-Romanesque, including a closed, squat structure with a leaning roof and three naves of more or less the same height, covered by indirectly lit barrel vaults (light came through the lateral walls, creating a mysterious ambience). Towers and a prominent westwork did not hold great importance in the region and they were often left out of the designs. That is not to say the area lacked towers completely, however. Saint-Front in Périgueux, and other isolated examples, such as the cathedral in Le Puy-en-Velay, show surprising inventiveness. In south-western France, there are roughly sixty churches with single naves covered with cupolas, for example in Périgueux, Le Puy, Cahors, Solignac and Souillac. On each bay, a dome based on a scheme that was familiar in other regions, including Puglia, the grandiose towers in Salamanca, Spain, and in the very special case of St Mark's in Venice.

Conversely, in the Midi region of France, the compositional problems with principal façades and entrance façades were resolved in a different way. Indeed, provincial architects ceased to employ their common Romanesque portals and looked directly to the Classical forms of ancient Roman monuments that still existed in the region. They then applied their own free interpretations to create structures such as the Church of St Trophime in Arles, and the formidable portals at the abbey church in Saint-Gilles-du-Gard.

Abbey church in Saint-Gilles-du-Gard, France, circa 1170

In southern France, especially in the provinces of Provence and Languedoc, where there are still plentiful ruins from antiquity, many of the façades have been inspired by ancient Roman monuments: here the triumphal west portal.

THE MASTERPIECE
THE BASILICA OF ST MARY MAGDALENE, VÉZELAY

This basilica was dedicated to Mary Magdalene and is still an important pilgrimage destination as a home to the relics of the saint. It is also the starting point of one of the French routes to Santiago de Compostela in north-western Spain. St Mary Magdalene was built in three different stages: the aisles and the nave between 1104 and circa 1132, the narthex on two levels between 1135 and 1151, and the transept and the Gothic chancel between 1190 and 1215. It later underwent comprehensive restoration by architect Viollet-le-Duc between 1840 and 1859. The west façade, from the same period as the narthex, was never completed. The church has an unaltered, elongated, Romanesque plan that aimed at bringing back a simple and essential church structure by basically eliminating the matroneum above the aisles. Beyond its administrative dependence on Cluny, the basilica was not under the direct influence of the mother church; it thus maintained its regional Burgundian features, such as the raised cross vaults with sharp edges, both in the nave and in the aisles. The result is a perfect model for a three-aisled basilica with huge transverse arcades and direct light that emphasises the overall chiaroscuro effects of the building.

opposite page
The nave of the Basilica of St Mary Magdalene, Vézelay, France, circa 1104–1132

In contrast to Cluny's focus on the vertical, this nave has a strong longitudinal development with an impressive horizontal effect due to the accentuated width and the simple two-level partitions, marked by a robust horizontal cornice – the elimination of the matroneum allowed for tall window openings. The main features of the nave include: the harmonious sequence of bays, created by large transverse arches, and the large, alternating, bichromatic blocks that decorate the faces of the arches, friezes, ribbons and racemes (ornamental motifs in clusters of branches, flowers and leaves), which lend a decorative quality to architectural elements such as the arcades, the windows and the various levels of the walls. All this creates an effect of extreme clarity and an atmosphere of rare beauty, amplified by the intense lighting.

Central portal of the Basilica of St Mary Magdalene, Vézelay, France, circa 1104–1132

The portals and capitals here are among the greatest achievements of Romanesque sculpture in the first half of the 12th century. Indeed, the basilica in Vézelay is home to an architectural and decorative innovation: the trumeau, a sculpted central pilaster that divides the entrance into two. The images of the central double portal present rare iconographic themes as well: the Pentecost with the descent of the Holy Spirit, and the apostles being sent to spread the "good news" – powerful images in the era of the Crusades, when each Christian had a duty to spread to the Gospel.

THE MASTERPIECE
THE CHURCH OF ST TROPHIME, ARLES

Sculptural architecture in the Provence region reached its apex in the façade and cloister of the Church of St Trophime in Arles. Dating from the second half of the 12th century, this building, like Saint-Gilles-du-Gard, merges impressive Toulousain tradition and new Provençal forms, characterised by total adherence to the canons of Classical statuary. Arles had been the capital of southern France since late antiquity, and thus represented an important centre for the conservation of holy relics, especially in the 12th century. The relics of Bishop Trophime, supposedly a disciple of St Peter, were transferred to the site in 1152. Built on a pre-existing basilica, the church has a high nave with a barrel vault flanked by narrow aisles, as shown in the salient-shaped exterior façade. The façade represents a wonderful architectural solution that develops an iconographic excellence in the narrative friezes of the portal.

opposite page
View of the cloister in the Church of St Trophime, Arles, France, circa 1150–1190

This cloister, which was built in two separate phases, is specifically Romanesque in the northern and eastern parts, which are the two parts closest to the church. Structured on pairs of columns with magnificent sculpted capitals, and with pilasters embellished with religious stories, the cloister at Arles draws on styles from antiquity and demonstrates the will of the Romanesque sculptors to emulate ancient Rome. In the background is the three-storey bell tower marked by string courses.

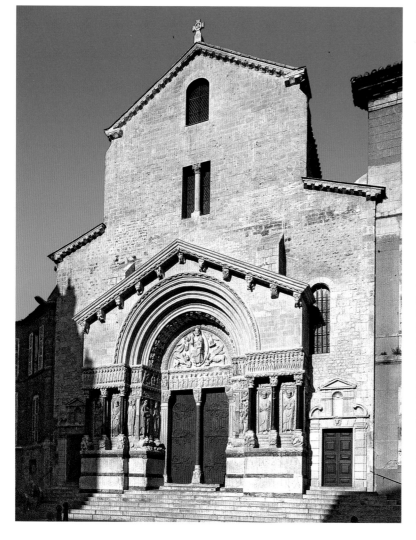

The façade of the Church of St Trophime, Arles, France, circa 1150–1170

On the high foundation, one can see lions with their prey while the sculpted bases support columns with likewise sculpted capitals featuring foliage motifs. Big statues of apostles and archangels are placed between the pilasters of the portal, and the dense frieze above bears images of the blessed and the damned. The portal is elegantly divided by a single column that supports the architrave and shows the twelve apostles. The tympanum features Jesus surrounded by the angel, the lion, the bull and the eagle (the "four living beings", or the tetramorph – representations of the four evangelists).

THE IBERIAN PENINSULA

In Spain and Portugal, the arrival and spread of Romanesque architecture developed differently than in most other western European countries. On the one hand, it was closely linked to the process of reconquering territories occupied by the Moors; on the other hand, it focused on the pilgrimage site of Santiago de Compostela in the north-west. The southern regions were under the more advanced cultural rule of the Moors, who had a profound influence on architectural styles, while the importance of the pilgrimage route to Santiago explains the presence of French influence in the area. The co-existence of Christian and Muslim civilisations on the Iberian Peninsula naturally led to a variety of communities co-existing closely together.

After being "reconquered" by Alfonso VI of Castile in 1088, Ávila, for example, became a centre of economic activity enlivened by the arrival of Christians, Jews and Moriscos (converted muslims) escaping persecution in southern Spain. Declared a World Heritage Site by UNESCO, Ávila is the only city with Romanesque city walls that are still fully intact, including its towers and gates. Built at the end of the 11th century, under the initiative of Alfonso VI, the walls were reconstructed starting in 1596, on the orders of Philip II. The imposing nature of the defensive system was justified by its geographical position and was a direct result of purely military motives: the city was in a borderland territory that was continually under attack from the Moors.

La Vera Cruz, Segovia, Spain, consecrated in 1208

The Church of La Vera Cruz (the True Cross) was probably built on the orders of the Knights of the Holy Sepulchre to house a fragment of the Sacred Cross, which was used for their investitures. The central chapel has blind walls and protrudes above the roof in order to draw in light from highly placed windows.

The rise of chivalric orders in Spain and Portugal was directly related to the route to Santiago. According to legend, the Reconquista received some help from St James (after which he was given the name "Matamoros", lit. "Moor slayer") when he "miraculously" appeared in the Battle of Clavijo (near Compostela) in 844, and helped the Christians fend off Moorish advances in Galicia. The military efforts of knights were repaid by their sovereigns with gifts of land, which led to a compact network of castles and military fortifications in strategic positions around the Portuguese and Spanish kingdoms. They were often along the banks of rivers or near the sites liberated from Moorish control. The castles belonging to the Knights Templar included Ponferrada, Almansa, Belmont, Peñiscola, Miravet and, lastly, Tomar, in Portugal. The latter continued to grow around its Romanesque nucleus until, at the beginning of the 16th century, it took on the spectacular appearance of a fortified abbey. Inside many military structures from this era, one often finds interesting elements of religious architecture.

The oldest chivalric orders, the Hierosolymitani (Order of the Holy Sepulchre) and the Knights Templars, integrated not only elements from France and local architecture into their architectural creations, but also recaptured motifs from the Holy Land, giving a cosmopolitan appearance to contemporary works. As a result, the Iberian Peninsula between the 11th and 13th century became home to a series of original buildings that had taken the Church of the Holy Sepulchre in Jerusalem as their model.

The walls of Ávila, Spain, end of the 11th century

Rising over a relatively flat terrain, the city walls in Ávila encircle an irregular rectangular area and feature 88 defensive towers. It is one of the major works of fortification in Castile from the 11th century. Atop the 12-metre-high (40-foot) wall is a walkway, and every 20 metres (66 feet), there is a semicircular tower, a feature that distinguishes the Castilian fortifications from those in the rest of Europe. The fortified walls are built of stone and mortar and the towers are integrated into the walls; the defensive aspect of the fortification is emphasised by its crenellation.

LOMBARDY AND THE PO VALLEY

The great architecture of the Po Valley, before and after the turn of the 12th century, was exclusively Romanesque thanks to a constant exchange with France and northern and central Europe. The region developed not only in major centres, such as Milan and Pavia, but also along the roads leading to and from Rome. From both a structural and decorative point of view, the Romanesque architecture of Lombardy and Emilia was rich in regional and local variations, sharing several distinct yet common features. This led to the construction, for example, of completely barrel-vaulted structures between 1090 and 1120 – late compared to other areas – but Milanese master builders did introduce a feature that had a revolutionary aesthetic and structural impact: they raised the cusp of the vault and used the groin to differentiate the static function of the supporting ribs from that of the cells.

The cross-vaulted ceiling, the matronea, the apses with low galleries and the façades with large gables were the characteristic elements of Romanesque architecture in northern Italy, to which the uniquely Italian element of the "protiro" was added: a small portico (similar to a narthex) jutting out from the main portal and emphasising its function by projecting it from the façade to the opposite wall, thereby creating an intermediate "wrapping space" halfway between the actual portico and the splayed outer portal. Moreover, in the great churches of the Po Valley, the crypt created an increasingly intimate relationship with the main church by occupying nearly the whole transept: a solution adopted around the same time in Modena, at San Zeno in Verona, in Venice and also in areas of southern Italy.

opposite page
Façade of the Basilica of San Michele Maggiore, Pavia, first half of the 12th century

Romanesque architectural convention provided a variety of solutions for the exterior of churches. The most common was a peaked façade – divided into three vertical units – that reflected the structure of the nave and aisles. In Pavia, the basilicas of San Michele and San Pietro in Ciel d'Oro began the transformation of the façade into a wall placed in front of the west end, hiding the outline of the aisles and looking almost like a "screen" or a "gable". Yet, the typical Romanesque articulation of walls manifests itself in the piercing of the façade with corridors and galleries, semicolumns, cornices, niches, sequences of ranging arcades and arches, and in the rich architectural decoration and formal rhythm of the windows and portals.

Apse of the Basilica of Santa Maria Maggiore, Bergamo, 1157

Construction on Santa Maria Maggiore began in 1157 and was the work of master builder Fredo. By 1187, before works were held up due to financial difficulties, the presbytery and the eastern apses were complete. They are structured into two levels: the first with deeply splayed windows, the second with a small gallery (a passage flanked on the outside by an uninterrupted series of small arcades with columns) on columns with Corinthian capitals.

THE MASTERPIECE
THE BASILICA OF SANT'AMBROGIO, MILAN

Sant'Ambrogio has been the religious and cultural heart of Milan since early-Christian times, but the current building is the result of a radical Romanesque transformation that took place when the city became a free duchy. The basilica incorporates significant parts of the previous early-Christian structure, altered in the Carolingian era (9th century) with the addition of a blind nave. Compared to the spatial structure of the churches along the pilgrim routes in south-western Europe, the aesthetic result here is quite different: Sant'Ambrogio changes the proportions drastically and abandons the effects of verticality in order to adopt a lower, wider shape. The masterly, creative solution of a gabled façade with a portico and a loggia above it, both with arcades, perfectly corresponds to the internal partition, and at the same time suggests the simplified scheme of a triumphal Roman arch, lending the façade a symbolic meaning as a glorious entrance to God's house. Access to the basilica is via a characteristic four-sided portico (quadriporticus) that draws on the character of ancient Roman building and the atria of early-Christian architecture. It also fulfils the functions of a monumental entrance and a space for religious and secular meetings. Thanks to itinerant master builders, the architectural solutions used for Milan's main basilica were not only applied throughout Lombardy, but also well beyond, and it is to them that we owe the spread of embellishments such as Lombard bands, blind arcades and false or accessible loggias that animate the surface of the walls.

opposite page
View of the atrium and façade of the Basilica of Sant'Ambrogio, Milan

Nave of the Basilica of Sant'Ambrogio, Milan

The interior of Sant'Ambrogio, comprising a body with a nave and two aisles without a transept but with a deep apse, is characterised by a sequence of four large bays supported by strong pilasters. The matroneum above the aisles looks out over the nave and has wide, round arches. The perspective focuses on the exceptional altar covered in gold leaf – a masterpiece of Carolingian goldsmiths (9th century) combined with a ciborium (canopy) supported by ancient columns of red porphyry (10th century).

THE MASTERPIECE
MODENA CATHEDRAL

The typology, construction methods, styles and decorative details used in the Basilica of Sant'Ambrogio in Milan were also applied to the cathedrals in the Emilia region. Together, they form a group of Romanesque buildings of extraordinary variety and importance. Modena Cathedral – begun in 1099, consecrated in 1184 and completed in the 13th century – comprises a simple body on a rectangular plan, without a transept and articulated in double bays on pilasters alternating with columns, false matronea to create depth, a large crypt and a raised presbytery. The ceiling was originally covered with trusses supported by transverse arches, but was later replaced by heavy, cross-ribbed vaults with pointed arches. The creator of this exceptional masterpiece was Lanfranco, whose originality consisted in adopting a figurative plan that was not yet Romanesque and translating it into a Romanesque language by going back to the motif of transverse arches supporting the roof – already seen

in Lomello. The architect rejected a vault concept, instead choosing an alternative to the Romanesque style of northern Italy, just as it was reaching its apex. Together with Lanfranco, another name must be cited here: Wiligelmo. He is responsible for the sculpted reliefs on the façade, an imaginative series of human figures and animals in which the narrative reliefs tell stories from Genesis. With the two funerary geniuses, and other items, the sculptor expresses a sorrowful and dramatic concept of man and his destiny. Within the space of a few years, the contemporary and convergent activity of the two artists brought the Romanesque to full maturity, with such originality that they are among the most significant achievements of the period. The apses and southern flank of the cathedral overlook the market square, hence the significance of the ancient units of measure on the exterior of the main apse: the cheese, the brick, the arm, the perch (or pole) and the tile.

Wiligelmo, *Expulsion from the Garden of Eden*, detail from Genesis, façade of Modena Cathedral, late 11th/early 12th century

Wiligelmo is the first great figure in Romanesque sculpture in Italy thanks to the complexity and richness of the themes he depicted: ancient stories of the Christian world depicted in a slow, calm and solemn manner. Against a neutral background, the sequence of the small blind arches here then gives a brief but effective spatial value in which the figures emerge, detaching themselves with great effort from the stone and taking on a primordial sturdiness, forever fixed in the vividness of the gestures that make the action immediately clear. The heavy physicality of the bodies communicates the sense of the gravity of the sin, the severity of the punishment and the toil of redemption through hard labour.

**opposite page
Exterior of Modena Cathedral**

Blind arches and an accessible loggia encircle this building and unify the façade, flanks and apse. The solution connects the alternation of linear elements with the chiaroscuro, sculpted articulation of the walls.

THE MASTERPIECE
THE BASILICA OF SAN ZENO, VERONA

San Zeno is home to the relics of the patron saint of this city. It stands on a large square, like many other churches in northern Italy, linking the religious significance of the site to the secular value of the free commune. The basilica, originally adjoining a Benedictine monastery, of which the cloister and a tower remain, adopts the same structural plans and compositional schemes as Modena, with a strict coherence between exterior and interior (a salient-shaped façade hints at the plan of the aisles and nave) and an articulation of the interior space in bays marked by pilasters. The trefoil-arched ceiling, like the bottom of a hull (end of the 14th century), replaced the original trussed ceiling. Outside, however, the treatment of the walls, divided by slender shafts, and the use of tuff stones coupled with horizontal courses in brickwork and marble inlays, produce a characteristic refined effect of light and colour that is reiterated in the tall, slender bell tower.

Interior of the Basilica of San Zeno, Verona, 10th–12th century

The system of supports alternates between solid pilasters and elegant columns. The use of pale building materials and the presence of windows in the upper section of the nave give the interior a pleasant, diffused light, which is rather unusual in Romanesque churches.

**Exterior of the Basilica
of San Zeno, Verona**

The exterior of San Zeno incorporates
some special features: the belfry with
a cusp, on the right, is an isolated
tower that is separate from the body
of the basilica; and on the left is a
brick tower with crenellation that
recalls the defensive structures that
protected the old Benedictine abbey.

THE VENETIAN LAGOON

Romanesque churches in the Venetian archipelago – from Venice to Grado – had features very different to those in the Po Valley; more than anywhere else, they maintained a firm loyalty to early-Christian and Byzantine styles and betrayed those from Ravenna. Venice, though independent from the Eastern Roman Empire since the 9th century, still had its economic and cultural focus in Byzantium, despite evidence of Lombardian roots. The churches of the Venetian Lagoon were often of ample size, with imposing bell towers built as reference points for seafarers. The gabled or tripartite façades (due to the height of the nave and side aisles) were rather simple, constructed of brick because of the soft soil, while the interiors (built on columns and covered with wooden frames) were very ornate, with elaborate capitals, shining mosaics and elegant inlaid floors.

The outstanding complex on the island of Torcello has a traditional pattern. The Cathedral of Santa Maria Assunta there features a basilica layout that is essentially taken from Ravenna: three naves divided by arcades of columns surmounted by recycled capitals, and extremely simple exterior decorations characterised by slender shafts. The design of the Church of Santa Fosca (circa 1011), meanwhile, was inspired by Byzantine models with a Greek cross plan surmounted by a cupola. The cupola was never completed. Adaptations of Lombard precedents in local styles can be found in the hinterland, in the Benedictine abbey of Pomposa. The church, built in a late-Ravenna style during the 8th and 9th centuries, was finally completed in the 11th century with the addition of an atrium flanked by an imposing bell tower.

opposite page
The central nave of the Cathedral of Santa Maria Assunta, Torcello, Venice, Italy, begun in 1008

The long walls here appear to hover weightlessly on long rows of columns; they are remnants of early-Christian styles. The splendid floor in marble inlay distinguishes the central nave chromatically and visually from the presbytery beyond the iconostasis (a structure that separates the presbytery from the nave, on which sacred images are displayed). The continuity of early-Christian elements can be traced back to both Veneto and Ravenna, while some more specifically Byzantine traits can be seen in the mosaics and the sculptural decoration, which was probably reused.

Exterior of the apse of the Cathedral of Santa Maria and San Donato, Murano, Venice, Italy, circa 1140

Murano Cathedral was originally dedicated to the Virgin, but after 1125, San Donato, whose body was secretly transported there from Cephalonia, was included in the honours. The whole area of the presbytery, dominated by the large apse and the pastophoria (side chambers), recalls Byzantine spatial relations and is clearly influenced by Lombardian elements in the two levels of loggias. The loggias, for their part, create effects of light and colour that offset the sculptural relief and produce a subtle transparency. The ornamental band in the exterior terracotta shows precious marble inlays while the brick walls feature blind arcades.

THE MASTERPIECE
THE BASILICA OF ST MARK, VENICE

St Mark's in Venice began as a place to store the alleged relics of Mark the Evangelist from Alexandria, Egypt, stolen by Venetian merchants in 828. Originally, it was a chapel inside the Doge's Palace and a shrine commemorating the martyrdom of the city's patron saint. As such, it gained a civic and celebratory role that inspired the rebuilding of the old location to reflect the power and wealth of the mighty maritime republic; the old church was demolished and a new one was built in 1063, during a time of cultural and artistic renewal. The church was consecrated in 1094, a date that signalled the end of construction and the beginning of a series of uninterrupted elaborations and renovations that would continue for centuries. Unique in the history of western Europe, 11th-century Venice remained substantially distanced from the artistic developments of the greater Padana area. So much so, in fact, that when the need arose to make formal and cultural choices with regard to the construction of the city's basilica, tastes inclined towards a model from five centuries earlier and located in Constantinople: the Basilica of the Holy Apostles. It was a way of affirming the alleged apostolic origins of the patriarchate of Venice. At the end of the 12th century, the original brick frontage was clad in sumptuous marble, with mosaics and rich sculptural decoration; the façade was even raised by two storeys of arches that were echoed by the profile of the domes.

Interior of Saint Mark's Basilica, Venice, Italy, consecrated in 1094

The interior of Saint Mark's still consists of the Byzantine building of the 6th century: five round domes on a Greek cruciform plan. The play of light and coloured marble walls combined with the gold-background mosaics seem to change the wall surfaces into pictorial values, denying any depth to the space.

**Exterior view of Saint Mark's
Basilica, Venice, Italy, 1094**

The narthex of Saint Mark's was
extended along the sides of the naves
in 1024, thus creating a wide atrium
surrounding the entire front section
of the basilica. The tympani of the
façade (the triangular frames above
the portal and windows) are in the
decorated Gothic style and were
added in the 15th century.

CENTRAL ITALY

The Apennine Mountains acted as a natural border between the Po Valley, home to the great development of Lombard Romanesque architecture, and the southern-central regions of Italy, where a variety of vernacular architecture flourished. Romanesque architecture in Tuscany, for example, differs from that of Lombardy, due to both diverse ideological premises and simple differences in taste; it converts the structural elements, the spatial relations, the dimensions and the volumes into tidy, flat surfaces with a rational harmony of geometric shapes.

There were two "schools" around which the autonomous and creative local architecture evolved. On the one hand was Florence, with its baptistery and Church of San Miniato; on the other hand was the cathedral in Pisa, which would inspire an extraordinary development in the 12th century. Common to both were polychrome marble cladding, especially on the exterior; together with the use of blind arches, this was the distinguishing mark of Tuscan Romanesque architecture, from the Badia in Fiesole to the parish

The central nave of San Miniato al Monte, Florence, Italy, 1028–1062

San Miniato seems to have only cautiously adopted the innovations of Romanesque architecture, instead preferring to maintain more Classical and early-Christian models, with recycled Corinthian-capital columns and a ceiling with wooden trusses. The Romanesque style was ultimately adopted in the transverse arches and the raised crypt. The heavy walls become lighter with the help of colourful insets: surfaces are covered with white and green geometrical motifs that elegantly underline the various architectural features.

Northern elevation of San Giovanni Fuorcivitas, Pistoia, Italy, 12th century

The exterior of the northern side of this church features colourful horizontal stripes of white marble and green serpentine, which actually distracts from the alternating arcades and blind arches on the various levels.

church at Empoli and San Giovanni Fuorcivitas in Pistoia. Beyond Tuscany, the range of Romanesque architecture in central Italy was limited in its quality and originality. The distinctive feature until the middle of the 13th century was a lack of stone vaults, which constituted an almost insurmountable obstacle with regard to renovations and often restricted patrons and builders to the traditional forms of basilicas, with pilasters or columns and a roof covering. The swift influence of models created in Pisa, a direct consequence of the economic and political dominance of the city, was seen in a series of works in the Tuscan hinterland and in the Tyrrhenian islands. Lucca, another flourishing commercial centre, was part of this artistic renewal as well, with several new buildings characterised by a severe Classicism, among them the Church of Sant'Alessandro. But starting in the 12th century, the influence of Pisa was paramount in basilica design, in particular in terms of interiors and façades, with rows of open galleries, such as those at the Cathedral of St Martin and the Church of San Michele in Foro. Still, the "Lucchese" interpretation can be seen in the contrasting masses, chiaroscuro elements and polychromatic inlay work. The same features appeared in Pistoia, in the exterior decoration of San Giovanni Fuorcivitas, and in Arezzo, in the façade of Santa Maria della Pieve (12th/13th centuries), where the rows of open galleries created greater impact because of the use of sandstone without chromatic embellishments. Sardinia and Corsica were also influenced by the Romanesque of Pisa in the 12th century; it prevailed over all other trends (Provençal, Lombard, Arab and Byzantine). Such buildings were characterised by an emphasis on mass and volume by contrasting chromatic facings with local volcanic rock such as basalt and trachyte.

Church of San Pietro, Tuscania, Italy, beginning of the 13th century

With a surprising display of Etruscan and Roman sarcophagi, the Church of San Pietro in Tuscania presents a bare and solemn basilica plan with three naves, a ceiling with wooden trusses and columns with capitals that were recycled from earlier buildings, a reminder of ancient early-Christian basilicas. The bases of the columns are joined by stone seats that run along the whole nave.

**opposite page
San Michele in Foro, Lucca, Italy, 11th/12th centuries**

Rising on the location of an old Roman forum, San Michele stands isolated in the urban landscape. Its tall façade is partitioned vertically into five orders of loggias, which follow the model of the cathedral in Pisa – a model already adopted for St Martin's in Lucca, interpreted here with rich decoration, colours and chiaroscuro styling in the marble inlays to create a bicolour effect to complement the sculptural relief of the architecture.

THE MASTERPIECE
PIAZZA DEI MIRACOLI, PISA

In 1063, the Maritime Republic of Pisa defeated the Moors at Palermo and gained control of the Mediterranean; the substantial loot they were able to collect went to funding the construction of the new cathedral, built on the outskirts of the old town, safe from flooding caused by the Arno. Planned by Buscheto at first, then by Rainaldo (who enlarged the nave and designed the façade), it was a building without parallel in its time – in fact, it was not complete at the time of its consecration in 1118. The exceptional character of this monument lies in the overall structure, soundly placed at the centre of a large urban space with proportions that harmonise with the other architectural elements of the monumental complex: the baptistery, the tower and the cemetery. The articulation of the exterior of the cathedral is characterized by an uninterrupted band of blind arcades – tall, narrow, embellished with refined marble inlays and with a decorative motif of Armenian origin, consisting of lozenges inside the round arches. The band runs all the way around the sides of the main basilica body, the transept and the chancel. The play of colours and the alternation of surfaces culminate in the splendid and rich façade of delicately coloured sandstone, decorated with glass and majolica sheets, and with marble knots, flowers and animals. The upper part is one of the most playful solutions the Romanesque period ever saw in terms of the façade harmonising with the body of the church: the flat surface disappears, pierced by four levels of passable galleries that interpret the Lombard loggias with additional colours and light. This weft creates a transparent façade to great pictorial effect.

opposite page
The central nave of St Mary of the Assumption Cathedral, Pisa, Italy, consecrated in 1118

The cathedral is a monumental cruciform-shaped structure with five aisles, matronea, a large transept and a dome with an oval base rising on the crossing. The echo of the great early-Christian, Roman churches with columns is diminished by its height, accentuated by the ogival (pointed) triumphal arch separating the nave from the presbytery. The motifs of the Classical tradition (the columns and capitals), of the early-Christian tradition (the ground plan) and of the oriental tradition (the ogive, the oval dome and the decoration in black-and-white stripes) merge harmoniously with the spatial proportions of the Romanesque.

View of the Piazza dei Miracoli with baptistery, cathedral and tower, Pisa, Italy, 11th–13th centuries

The baptistery in Pisa fits into the mould of refined decoration and the cultured elaboration of various influences. It was created by architect Deotisalvi in 1152 as a large cylinder standing harmoniously in front of the church on the same axis of symmetry. Like the cathedral, it is marked by a series of blind arcades and decorated with motifs from ancient and Oriental tradition. The well-known tower was begun in 1173 (the architect is unclear), but only completed towards the end of the 14th century – work was delayed by a sinking foundation. The tower presents the same figurative themes and architectural features as the cathedral and the baptistery, with the same positive results, amplified by the visual effect from changes in perspective and chiaroscuro created by the perforated circular shape.

THE MASTERPIECE
THE ABBEY OF SANT'ANTIMO

Built in the 12th century, in the province of Siena at the foot of Monte Amiata, Sant'Antimo is a masterpiece among the great Italian Benedictine monasteries. Located on the ancient via Francigena, it can be compared to Cluny for its isolated position and dimensions; it was also one of the richest and most powerful Italian monasteries. Despite the affluence it enjoyed, however, Sant'Antimo embraced formal principles and a simple style of building that expressed a sensibility in line with the spiritual aspirations of the monastic reformation of the 11th and 12th centuries.

below and opposite page
Abbey of Sant'Antimo, Castelnuovo dell'Abate, Siena, 12th century
The interior has a basilica ground plan ending in a chancel with an ambulatory and radial chapels where the influence of the French pilgrim churches is recognisable. Columns alternating with pilasters separate the central nave, covered with wooden trusses, from the side aisles with matronea. In the chancel is a circle of simple Corinthian-capital columns with a double series of foliage resembling later Gothic capitals, with curling leaves (crochet) of French derivation; conversely, the abacus (upper part of the capital) features abstract and geometrical decorations.

ROME, PAPAL CITY

With its passive loyalty to early-Christian and Byzantine basilica models, Rome lived in a sort of static conservatism, barely influenced by the otherwise dominant architectural culture of Lombardy, which in Rome only affected the reconstruction of bell towers. This continued for the entire Romanesque period, justified perhaps by a desire to express religious fervour by replicating the architectural forms of the original churches. The papal city remained the centre of all attempts to revive the traditions of antiquity, which seemed to have laid claim to an ideological and political legacy here.

The attitude of extreme conservatism among papal patrons resulted in the Roman architecture becoming an uninspired imitation of models from late antiquity, even in the 13th century. The most innovative and impressive results appear in the cloisters of St John Lateran and St Paul Outside the Walls, where families of craftsmen – Cosmati and Vassalletto, in particular – created a series of authentic, Classical forms dignified by the reuse of valuable materials with Islamic and Byzantine influences.

below left
Basilica of Santa Maria in Cosmedin, Rome, Italy, 12th century

Church exteriors in Rome in the 12th century were characterised by clear, sharp surfaces delicately highlighted by shafts, arcades and Classical toothed cornices. The simple structures of an atrium with portico adjoin the façades, creating an entrance to the church that is open but protected. The bell towers show an original Roman elaboration of Lombardian forms, lightened by an increasing number of openings and decorated with elegant horizontal string courses and polychrome cups of majolica inserted occasionally in the brick wall.

opposite page, right
Detail of the cloister at the
Basilica of St John Lateran,
Rome, Italy, 1215–1232

Opposite the entrance to the porch,
an inscription bears the names of the
builders of the cloister: members of
the famous Vassalletto family, Roman
mosaic artists that were active in
the 12th and the 13th centuries. At
St John Lateran they achieved a
masterpiece of compositional balance
thanks to the extremely rich mosaic
and inlay decoration of the elegant
columns, with alternately smooth
or coiled surfaces that reveal
Byzantine influences.

above
Exterior of the Basilica
of San Clemente, Rome, Italy,
1099–1118

This basilica shows motifs seen in
the Constantinian basilicas. It is
divided by marble columns into three
naves and the decoration, by Roman
mosaic artists, is one of the most
comprehensive and lavish still in
existence. It includes a Cosmatesque
floor, with inlays of porphyry and
serpentine roundels, the screen of
the schola cantorum (area reserved
for the choristers) which reuses
elements from the 6th century,
two pulpits, the beautiful "woven"
candelabra, the Classical ciborium
(a canopy standing over the altar
and supported by four columns)
and the episcopal chair.

THE ROMANESQUE IN PUGLIA

Byzantine architectural culture – tinged with Moorish influences – was very persistent in the regions of southern Italy. The other major influence here was Benedictine monastic architecture. In Puglia, for example, which was recaptured from the Moors at the end of the 11th century, the Byzantine tradition was so deeply rooted that it survived even the Norman conquest. In fact, playing the natural role of "stepping stone" between the Orient and Europe, the cities along the coast of southern Italy flourished during the years of Norman dominance. The period witnessed major urban renewal and the construction of lavish cathedrals. Important Lombardian influences were also embraced by itinerant master builders. Even if the most important period of Romanesque architecture in Puglia began with the construction of the Basilica of San Nicola in Bari, and continued with the creation of monumental cathedrals in the 12th century – at Trani, Troia and Ruvi – Puglia's artistic scene had already been active in the preceding century. That phase was more sensitive to the preservation of Byzantine architecture, which resulted in the creation of churches of notable refinement, such as the Basilica of Santa Maria in Siponto, or smaller rural churches, such as the one at Seppannibale.

opposite page
Trani Cathedral, Trani, Italy, 1099–1222

Flanked by the imposing bell tower, this cathedral stands right on the waterfront, tall and perfect in its form, extraordinary unity and simplicity. The existence of a large crypt of the same dimensions as the church above gives the impression of a double church. The salient-shaped façade is pierced by a rose window that is surrounded by zoomorphic sculptures. The richly decorated portal opens at the mid-point of a sequence of blind arches.

Basilica of San Nicola, Bari, Italy, 1087–1105

The first of the great Romanesque churches in Puglia, San Nicola was built on the ruins of a Byzantine governor's palace. Its purpose was to house the relics of San Nicola that had been secretly taken by the Normans from Myra (now Turkey). It is the focus of religious and civic life in a town considered the strategic centre of the Latinisation of southern Italy. Compared to the primarily Byzantine features of 11th-century Puglian churches, San Nicola is compact and solid, more like a fortress. The façade features a Lombardian band at the top and blind arches at the base, and it is nestled between two powerful towers of Norman derivation. The "block" effect is further enhanced by the deep arcades, which, on the flanks of the church, connect the façade and the transept and are surmounted by a shallow loggia; the motif is reminiscent of similar solutions from ancient Rome or late antiquity and is widespread in the Puglian buildings of the 11th and 12th centuries.

THE ARAB-NORMAN STYLE IN SICILY

After two centuries of Moorish dominance, the Norman conquest of Sicily brought the island back into the European fold. Upon arriving in Sicily, the Normans found a figurative and architectural cultural legacy greatly influenced by Byzantine forms and Islamic decorative styles. Faced with such sophisticated modes of expression, the new rulers made every effort – and with great success – to assimilate. This gave rise to numerous works of high artistic quality that were produced in roughly seventy years, between 1130 and 1200. The dominant thrust of Sicilian architecture in the 12th century was to pay maximum possible attention to the crossing (the area between the nave and the transept), making it the nucleus of the church by using the effects of perspective and chiaroscuro. Halfway through the 12th century, a few late-Romanesque elements worked their way in: rich, exaggerated articulation of the church exterior, especially of apses; Moorish-style roofing with a stellar vault; decoration using stone inlays; and stalactite-like formations on the ceilings.

The extraordinary variety and provenance of these decorative elements, including those of Byzantine, Islamic and Catalan-Provençal origin, reveal the eclecticism of this courtly repertoire. Several civic structures must also be taken into consideration here that are unparalleled in their number and typology in mainland Italy. The palaces, suburban villas, pavilions and kiosks, for example, such as the Torre Pisana in the Palazzo Reale at Palermo, or the summer residences, such as La Zisa and La Cuba, display cubic forms arranged in an axial and symmetrical style of undoubtedly Islamic origin.

opposite page
Palatine Chapel, Palermo, Italy, 1132–1143

The Palatine Chapel, which was the oratory of the royal palace, merges the model of a basilica, with three naves and columns, to a centrally planned presbytery crowned by a dome of Islamic derivation. The type and shapes of the wooden ceiling, with "stalactites" and "alveoli", were also heavily influenced by mosques in North Africa; they would reach their apex of decorative splendour in the later ceilings of the Alhambra in Granada. Columns and capitals date back to the Classical era; mosaics cover the interior spaces completely and are the work of Byzantine artists. The ambo was done by Romanesque sculptors. The variety of motifs and styles here is a testimony to the artistic and cultural syncretism of the Normans. The resplendent chapel features a rich fusion of forms, light and colours that create a unique atmosphere of aristocratic refinement.

La Zisa, Palermo, Italy, 1164–1180

Built by Arab artisans on orders from King William I (1122–1166) in the large hunting ground of "gennet-ol-ardh" (meaning "paradise on earth" and commonly called "Genoard"), La Zisa – from the Arabic al-aziz (meaning "noble, wonderful") – is a sumptuous palace nestled in grand gardens and irrigated by fountains and artificial lakes that were also used as ornamental fish ponds. From the outside, it is a compact block with an understated pattern of cornices and horizontal string courses. The three arches on the ground floor open onto the fish pond.

THE MASTERPIECE
MONREALE CATHEDRAL, PALERMO

Begun in 1172, on orders from King William II (1155–1189), Monreale is an imposing complex built on an elevated site – a grandiose symbol of the absolute power and magnificence of the Norman monarchy. The solemn spatiality of the church, which was intended to house the tombs of the kings, has a basilican plan with a T-shape modeled on the Abbey of Monte Cassino. The presbytery offers an original solution, with the addition of a wide, non-protruding transept; the result is a configuration much like a centrally planned church.

Façade of Monreale Cathedral, Palermo, Italy, begun in 1172

opposite page
Exterior of the apse of Monreale Cathedral, Palermo, Italy

This cathedral's exterior shows the influence of Islamic master builders: the neat, interlocking volumes of the apses and the colouring of the pointed blind arches, which are narrow, tall and criss-crossing.

This search for the maximum decorative effect is enhanced by the use of polychrome stones that change depending on the light. The same effect can be seen in gold mosaics inside the cathedral, which are inspired by Byzantine styles. All these heterogeneous elements are merged in a work of great fascination and equilibrium, a masterpiece of Norman eclecticism that is also complemented by the renowned cloister adjacent to the cathedral.

THE GERMAN TERRITORIES OF THE HOLY ROMAN EMPIRE

Due to the Investiture Controversy, the Holy Roman Empire experienced a period of political instability starting around 1076. This was then reflected in German architectural history. The Ottonian tradition remained anchored in its historic and cultural motivations, increasing the divide between the ideological conception of imperial basilicas and the new image of Romanesque churches. In fact, German territories were the last to adopt the principles of the late Romanesque, with churches constructed and adapted for stone vaults appearing only after 1080. After the first half of the 12th century, architectural trends broke with tradition, adopting a basilica with a roof supported on columns. At the same time, a series of grand cathedrals along the Rhine – at Speyer, Mainz, Koblenz and, later, Worms – maintained the German-style ground plan with choirs and lateral entrances. It was a rejection of the view of the interior that went from the entrance along the axis up to the apse. Yet, despite continued use of Ottonian forms of interior design, even conservative projects saw new developments on the exteriors, with massive blocks that accentuated values of pure geometry and structural simplicity. In this way, 12th-century German architecture, which had not yet adopted vaulted churches, aligned itself with the Romanesque, based on an aspiration to assign the same importance and quality to exteriors as to interiors. From the beginning of the medieval period, imperial courts lived in palaces. These imperial and royal palaces, with great halls, "ambulacri" (corridors located behind the altars or surrounding an apse), chapels and

opposite page
Maria Laach Abbey, Koblenz, Germany, begun in 1093

The beautiful exterior of the Benedictine church at Maria Laach Abbey, begun in 1093, shows a similarity of form and decoration to Speyer and Mainz cathedrals: two groups of towers of different shapes rise to the east and west, balancing each other and underlining the double aspect of the building. The decoration, however, consists of thin frames designed in a calligraphic style, with a playful alternation of colours; when viewing the whole, one feels a split between the architectural volumes and the ornamentation.

The Kaiserpfalz (Imperial Palace), in Gelnhausen, Germany, middle of the 12th century

The ruins of the Kaiserpfalz at Gelnhausen show a high level of refinement in the regular courses of cut stone; the walls are elegantly perforated with arcades.

atriums, were scattered across the entire territory, which at the time did not envisage fixed government seats. The storage houses connected to them were used for foodstuffs for the court; various parts of the construction as well as their functional design managed to revive Roman, Byzantine and German models.

The Kaiserpfalz (Imperial Palace) in Goslar was the seat of the imperial "diets" – a name adopted in the Middle Ages for certain political assemblies. It was first built in the Salian period (11th century) and later renovated between 1138 and 1268 by the Hohenstaufen dynasty. It is a prime example of a fortified palace in the Carolingian tradition, with annexed buildings erected under Henry II (1015–1019). The majority of the work, however, was completed under Henry III (1026–1056), halfway through the 11th century, with the construction of the apartments and the collegiate church, later transformed by Barbarossa (1152–1190) with the construction of the Chapel of Saint Ulrich. The ruins of the Kaiserpfalz in Gelnhausen, mentioned for the first time in 1158, is one of the most beautiful and artistically significant buildings in Germany. It served as living quarters for numerous German emperors, and was also the seat of several imperial diets. It was restored in the 19th century.

opposite page
Basilica of St Godehard,
Hildesheim, Germany, 1133–1172

This Saxon basilica in Hildesheim not only incorporated, but also further developed the characteristic elements of traditional Ottonian architecture: a basilica with opposing chancels, columns alternating with pilasters and flat roofing. The smooth walls are subtly interrupted by a thin cornice.

The Kaiserpfalz (Imperial Palace)
in Goslar, Germany, circa 1050

The impressive palace complex at Goslar groups a number of different elements into in a single block. The so-called imperial house, built in the middle of the 11th century, was radically transformed in the second half of the 19th century.

THE ROMANESQUE STYLE IN BRICK

A number of impressive Romanesque constructions were erected during the second half of the 12th century, in the territories between the Elbe and the Oder rivers. Indeed, around 1150, along the northern borders of the empire, the expansion of territory and political power was accompanied by the spread of Christianity and Christian art. Here, like in Spain, with its Moorish and Islamic influences, or in Italy with its Byzantine and Eastern Christian Church tradition, the indigenous population and their pagan cults were either pushed eastward, or converted and assimilated. It was not merely a question of military conquest, therefore, but also one of economic and social expansion that envisaged the foundation of new cities.

The area, traditionally denuded of its stone quarries, became reliant on brick as a building material, and it was used in both religious and secular architecture. Following the decline of the ancient Rome, brickwork was no longer common in Germany, but it experienced a rebirth in the Gothic architecture of northern Germany and around the fringes of the Baltic Sea. It came to characterise the monumental and urban image of German trading centres, Scandinavian cities and Baltic settlements linked to the Hanseatic League.

Jerichow Abbey Church, Germany, 1150–1190

Jerichow Abbey Church is the first example of a building of such dimensions constructed entirely of bricks: the cross-shaped basilica, amplified by the dazzling red colour, is built on columns with a flat ceiling, a raised bridge of the chancel and three apses, following the tradition of Benedictine churches. The extent of the crypt and the elevation of the chancel transform the interior into a sort of stage, high above the elongated body of the church.

Exterior of Jerichow
Abbey Church, Germany

SCANDINAVIA

The history of Romanesque architecture is not limited to western Europe. Mention must be made of the structures that fall within the style of northern Romanesque, in Denmark, Norway and Sweden. Up until the middle of the 11th century, buildings in Denmark were constructed in wood, but from that date forward, stone and brick were also used. From what can be seen in the fragments that survived later Gothic adaptations, the Danish Romanesque provided some notable examples, such as the fortified Church of Our Lady in Kalundborg, and the unique, multi-storey round churches at Nyker, Olsker, Nylarsker and Osterlasker, which were at once religious and defensive buildings. Norway's conversion to Christianity, which only began at the end of the 10th century, was completed by about 1000, with the unification of the Kingdom by Olaf II (1015–1028). As such, few Romanesque churches survive in that country: the cathedrals at Stavanger (begun in 1125) and at Trondheim, both of which were influenced by British architecture; the remains of the cathedral at Bergen (an ex-Franciscan church); and numerous small churches in stone built after 1100, among them Gamle Akers in Oslo. The most valuable secular building in Scandinavia is also in Bergen: the hall of King Håkon (1217–1263), completed in 1261 in the Gothic style. Different influences were at work in Sweden, from the Rhenish imperial buildings, such as those at Lund, to the Burgundian ones imported by the Cistercian foundations. The mendicant religious orders (Dominicans and Franciscans) imported from Germany the use of bricks in buildings.

Lund Cathedral, Sweden, begun 1103

Monumental stone architecture began in southern Sweden with the construction of Lund Cathedral. Often compared to Speyer because of its surprisingly rich, decorative style and the layout of the crypt and the transept, it has an elongated body structured like a vaulted basilica. It was given a dramatic remodel during the 19th century.

Nidaros Cathedral, Trondheim, Norway, begun in 1070

At 102 metres (336 feet) in length, this is the longest church in Scandinavia. It has an octagonal main body intended for the burial of St Olav. The imposing "screen" façade – marked by various orders of arcades, side towers and a large, central rose window – resembles the façade of many British cathedrals.

BETWEEN ROMANESQUE AND GOTHIC

Abbott Suger consecrated the choir of the Basilica of Saint Denis in 1144. In stylistic terms, this date corresponds to the beginnings of a nascent Gothic style and, in northern France, to the first signs of a new sensibility and novel architectural principles that were the product of careful technical research for an increasingly high central nave. The new direction was inspired by several important trends in the Romanesque style, from the Cistercian abbey at Cluny to the great Ottonian cathedrals, and would give birth to a fresh way of creating and experiencing space. Yet, at the time, the spread of artistic developments in the Ile-de-France area was not exactly in line with similar dynamic changes across western Europe; Romanesque architecture, in its later forms, continued across the continent.

Furthermore, in France (especially Burgundy and the south-western regions), the latest developments of Romanesque art continued in parallel with the ascendancy of the Gothic style, and for the rest of the 12th century, earlier architectural forms continued to be actively practised. It was only around 1200 that the Romanesque style seemed to fade and new, Gothic forms were adopted in earnest. The systematic use of the ribbed crossing in the central nave, for example, as a replacement of the barrel vault, allowed builders to create larger areas of space, effectively making a departure from the cramped verticality of previous constructions. The new choir in the Basilica of St Mary Magdalene in Vézelay, Notre-Dame in Dijon, the cathedrals at Auxerre, Chalon-sur-Saone, Geneva and Lausanne, not to mention several Norman churches, were distinguished primarily by their lightness of construction, walls embellished with tracery and galleries situated in front of the windows in the central nave.

Chancel and ambulatory
of the Basilica of Saint Denis,
France, 1144

With these structures, Burgundian architecture became a vital link between conservative, late-Romanesque areas and the Gothic regions known as the "Domaine Royale". Similarly, in Germany and Italy, the Romanesque began waning as French Gothic began its ascent, yet it was marked by its own specific character and independent trends. If monumental and powerful forms were dominant in German territories, late-Romanesque architecture in Italy remained largely conservative. In Spain, between 1150 and the end of the 13th century, the expulsion of the Moors (pushed south on the Iberian Peninsula) corresponded with construction at several sites: the old cathedral of Salamanca and those at Zamora and Toro are characterised by massive ribbed vaults and famous domed round towers, or "ciborios", which rise above the crossing in an imaginative profusion of masses.

opposite page
Abbey church, Fécamp, France, begun in 1168

Norman churches that were begun or rebuilt in the last three decades of the 12th century revived the elevational scheme with tribunes (rows of columns), as used in that period in northern France, but the technique of building thick walls was not abandoned; the structures still had a heavy look to them. The abbey church at Fécamp can be called typically Norman due to its three-level articulation of the wall of the central nave, the presence of the matroneum and the internal tribune located in front of the clerestory windows. Aside from its pointed arches with sharp edges, the church maintained all the sturdiness of a Romanesque structure and even became a model for subsequent buildings in the region.

Heisterbach Abbey, Bonn, Germany, 1202–1237

The Cistercian abbey church at Heisterbach is a complex and elaborated organism that now lies partially in ruins. It represents a high point of late Romanesque art in the Rhine region due to its rich decoration. In the only surviving part of the structure, one can see designs of Burgundian origin that have been adapted to local styles: the semicircular apse has an ambulatory, nine chapels and a double order of colonnettes cut against the grain. The rich vaults are divided into segments by protruding ribs, elements that foreshadow the Gothic stellar vault and the ribbed vault similar to the early English Gothic.

Cistercian innovations

With the emergence of a monastic regime that promulgated a return to its modest origins, Bernard of Clairvaux became the leading advocate of a type of architecture that reflected the values of rigour and clarity. From the beginning, this building programme was dominated by a religious spirit opposed to the excessive adornment and dimensions of Cluny or Saint Denis. Greater economic restraint required a more functional monumentality. The Cistercian Order precociously adopted ogival cross vaulting, but this did not provide the clear and rigorous subdivision of space typically seen in Gothic cathedrals. As a result, the Cistercian architecture of the 12th century is defined as "reduced Gothic": in simple terms, "reduced" to technical function-ality and to a new, well-lit definition of space that also adopted forms of architectural decoration from non-monastic structures.

The first experiments in cross-vaulting with cusped arches were probably those of the capitular halls. From there, the new system of vaulting spread to apsidal chapels, transepts, aisles and finally to vast central naves. This splendid architectural development is accompanied by a severe limitation

View of the cloister and bell tower of the Abbey of Santa Maria di Rovegnano, Milan, 1135–1150

Their rigorous ethics allowed the Cistercians to rapidly expand across Europe, a fact demonstrated by the numerous monasteries around the continent. Their architectural design is innovative and clearly recognisable beyond just the use of local materials. The most famous Cistercian church in northern Italy is Chiaravalle, near Milan. It is characterised by the use of red brick that gives the building its powerful red colour. The imposing, octagonal, multi-tiered tower from the 14th century testifies to an increasingly flexible observance of Cistercian rules (which had already begun after the death of St Bernard) and marks a pivotal point for the architectural style.

of décor: no gold crosses, only wooden ones; only one candelabra, made of iron; all liturgical tools in copper or iron, except for the communion chalice, which must be gilded silver, not gold; frocks, robes and vestments only in wool, linen or hemp (the same for the altar cloth), not in sumptuous fabric or with gold or silver embroidery.

In 1150, the General Chapter of the Order forbade "sculptures or paintings in the churches and other areas of the monastery, because looking at them prevents good meditation and a discipline of religious gravity". Soon after, stone bell towers were forbidden; small wooden towers with a maximum of two bells were deemed sufficient. Only after the new apse at Pontigny (1185) were Cistercian architects able to abandon this simplicity and approach the sumptuous style of the great cathedrals. From this moment, they began adhering to Gothic styles, despite the inclusion of different forms and types. They did not design complex structures and, at the beginning at least, did not build towers rising from the crossing; or so-called harmonic façades (i.e., with regular vertical and horizontal divisions); or the bell towers forbidden by the Cistercian rule. The expansion of the order was sudden and striking. In the second half of the 12th century, the "simplified" Gothic adopted by the Cistercians was exported to distant lands, where this new Gothic was totally absent: to southern France, to Spain, Italy, Britain, the German territories and even to Poland and Hungary.

Fortified churches: religion and safeguarding the territory

The church was often the only permanent stone structure in villages or towns, which largely constituted wooden houses. It was therefore not only the centre of religious life but also assumed a number of other functions. Being connected to the main square, where markets took place, it hosted meetings and negotiations. Units of measure and weight were indicated on its walls. Its bell tower was also a civic tower and the church building, often fortified, was a shelter for the faithful from external threats. This was all the more natural because of the structure of the Romanesque church, which had thick, strong walls and was often surrounded by the walls of a cemetery. From the 12th century onwards, churches even took on the look of real fortresses, thanks to the addition of defensive structures such as walkways, earthworks (inclined surfaces at the foot of the walls in medieval fortifications), walls with trapdoors in the walkways and arrowslits or loopholes (narrow openings that allowed light weapons to be fired at enemies). The church tower – used as a lookout against enemies or to spot fires – became a keep.

Religious fortifications were widespread in France. They defended not only the church's treasures, which were often on the higher floors of the bell tower and difficult to reach, but also the population during the religious wars. During the Hundred Years' War (1337–1453), thousands of churches were transformed into fortifications by raising the walls and the roof and creating shelters above the ceiling of the nave and the choir. In other cases, for example at Ávila, churches were integrated into a much larger system of fortification, where the monument merged with the defenses. This phenomenon then spread throughout Europe and as far as the borders of the Islamic world – there are numerous fortified churches in Transylvania, for example, a distant outpost and bulwark of the Christian world.

opposite page
The Church of Our Lady, Kalundborg, Denmark, 1170–1190

The impressive Church of Our Lady in Kalundborg, on Zealand island, stands out amongst the fortified buildings around it. This centrally planned church in the form of a Greek cross is built of red brick and features five towers to symbolise the recent Christianisation of the country. Each one rises from its own polygonal apse. The central focal point is provided by a taller, square tower in the middle.

Convent of the Order of Christ (formerly Templars), Tomar, Portugal, second half of the 12th century

THE LATE ROMANESQUE IN GERMANY

The emergence of the German Romanesque was the natural result of a cultural process that manifested characteristics and processes originally from the German realm, and which expressed itself through a variety of independent influences. The movement corresponded to contemporary stages of the French Gothic, which, aside from the ease of exchange between the two countries, did not succeed in exercising a significant influence on religious architecture in the German world. The thriving late Romanesque along the Rhine coincided with the era of the Hohenstaufen dynasty, and expressed the same vision and attachment to earthly life so vividly described in chivalric poetry and in the lyrical poems of the Minnesänger and by the exuberant Frederick Barbarossa. Once again, the architecture of the High Rhine region developed in the shadow of great imperial cathedrals. The cathedrals at Worms and Mainz were given their final appearance while Speyer underwent certain modifications including late-Romanesque cupolas. The Rhenish late Romanesque displayed a decisive tendency toward monumentality and formal rigour, accentuated by the use of local sandstone, which had a wonderful red tone. Exterior architecture resumed, developing into the Germanic imperial tradition of buildings conceived as a single walled block dominating the surrounding space – the square masses of the naves and towers were redesigned as a contrast. In the third decade of the 13th century, however, Romanesque German architecture also began to fade. The introduction of Gothic forms was applied to traditional typologies without using the formal, "static" system of primitive Gothic.

opposite page
Interior of the Basilica of the Holy Apostles, Cologne, Germany, 1190–1219

This robust church is near the main market square and demonstrates the wide range of solutions used in Romanesque architecture in Cologne. This basilica is modelled on Norman churches with matronea.

Exterior of the Basilica of the Holy Apostles, Cologne, Germany

THE MASTERPIECE
WORMS CATHEDRAL

The last of the great Rhine cathedrals, Worms was built between 1171 and 1210 on the site of a previous Ottonian church – it presented the same scheme as Speyer, built one century earlier, but maintained the Germanic trend of two chancels at the east and west ends, in the Carolingian tradition. Built over a period of two centuries, this cathedral is testimony to an extraordinary originality of design and real creative capacity. Notwithstanding the traditional presence of two opposite apses, the overall composition is varied and full of movement: there is just one transept to the east, and the two chancels are totally different. An even stronger artistic statement lies in the exterior, with a definite concentration of mass at the two ends of the building. At one end is the bulky east

chancel, a cubic block protruding from the transept and enclosed between two circular towers. At the other end is the polygonal westwork – a typical late-Romanesque shape that replaces semi-circular apses with polygonal outlines and expresses highly symbolical values with the use of light, as in Gothic tradition. The longitudinal section shows the body of the naves covered with cross vaulting (hidden from the outside by the slopes of the roof). This dates from the decades before and after the turn of the 13th century, during a stylistic transition towards Gothic forms, although it draws on features of Ottonian Romanesque, with the multiple styles of blocks formed by clusters of columns and semicolumns, and the colossal proportions of the pilasters.

View of the exterior of Worms Cathedral (below) and west chancel (opposite page), Germany

THE MASTERPIECE
MAINZ CATHEDRAL

The reconstruction of the cathedral at Mainz between 1110 and 1137, which addressed the naves and the east chancel, belongs to the stylistic phase of the late Romanesque in Germany and is characterised by the special attention paid to the composition of the external façades. However, it was completed later, after 1181. The form of the imposing east chancel, despite less harmonious additions such as the tops of the towers, shows a great sculptural quality that is enhanced by the reddish colour of the sandstone. The contrast between the powerful bare wall, framed between two circular towers in the Ottonian style, and the central apse, ornamented with a gallery, create an austere and solemn effect. Mainz Cathedral was for centuries an exceptional workshop of Romanesque, Gothic and Renaissance sculpture, characteristic features being the tombs of the archbishops leaning on the pilasters of the central nave.

opposite page
Exterior of Mainz Cathedral, Germany, completed after 1181

A symbol of political power as well as of the power of the Catholic Church, Mainz Cathedral – together with the cathedrals in Worms and Speyer – is the foremost example of Rhenish Romanesque.

Interior of Mainz Cathedral, Germany

THE NORWEGIAN STAVE CHURCHES

Norway's most significant contribution to Romanesque architecture was the "stavkirker", or stave church, named for the wooden columns that support the central part of the nave and the roof. These wooden structures with palisades only existed in northern Europe. Of the one hundred or so built between the 11th and 12th century, only twenty-five remain. The stavkirker is a type of church in which the combination of mass and architectural volumes is quite unique, but the construction of the naves, the arcades, supported on cylindrical columns, the wooden staves, the articulation of levels and the tower-like elevations are directly derived from the religiuos architecture of south-western Europe. The walls are constructed from wooden planks positioned vertically between corner posts and extending up to the roof trusses. A series of vaulted archways encircle the building's exterior, and the roof surfaces are positioned at different levels, one surmounting the other. The most important examples of stave churches are in Urnes (1060–1150), Lom (built in the 11th century, modified in 1630) and Borgund (1150).

opposite page
Heddal Stave Church, Norway, 1242

The Heddal Stave Church was built in 1242 and is the largest of its kind in Norway. Its three belfries and the sixty-four sections of its tiered roof make it a true "wooden cathedral".

Exterior and section of the Borgund Stave Church, Norway, circa 1150

The Borgund Stave Church is the only one of its kind that has not changed since medieval times. Dedicated to the Apostle Andrew, whose cross motif runs along the area above the arcade, the church has a very simple interior lit up by a few small openings in the upper part of the walls. The interior has a ceiling comprising a system of trusses and false beams (either vertical or angled elements that support downward thrust), so thin as to be almost invisible in the semidarkness, which makes the church look even slimmer. Conversely, the exterior is richly decorated on the portals and the gables with wooden carvings of animals, vines, dragon heads, runic inscriptions and other typical elements of Romanesque imagery. The pitched roofs, on six tiers, are covered with pine boards.

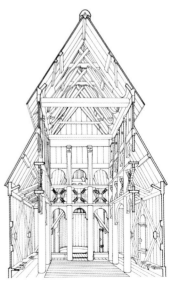

ITALY

Some areas in Europe lacked the dynamism of the Rhineland and Burgundy. Late-Romanesque architecture remained fairly conservative as a result. In Italy, and especially in central and southern regions, this tendency manifested itself above all in the flat ceilings of the basilicas, a trend that lasted for the whole 13th century. Vaulted churches were virtually unknown here, and the few that were built were completed under Cistercian patronage – the result was completely distanced from local traditions. The majority of flat-roofed basilicas continued late-Romanesque trends, but it is possible to date them based only on specific decorative features, such as forming cornices and ribs to accommodate enlarged cubic capitals. Nonetheless, in the late 12th century, vaulted ceilings became the norm across northern Italy, while the 13th century saw many forms adopted from northern France, such as pointed arches and six-sectioned vaults, albeit without having seen the dynamism with which these components were used north of the Alps. The range of styles reflects the expression of architectural choices made by a society with multiple social classes and different sources of patronage, from communal institutions to religious orders, and from the papacy to the empire. Nonetheless, besides rather conservative buildings, several original works of architecture emerged, thanks to which Italy, above all in the north but also elsewhere, assumed pole position in the development of late-Romanesque styles: the unique single-room churches in Piedmont, such as St Bernardo and St Mark in Vercelli, or the cathedral at Molfetta in Puglia, where the typology of the single-room church merged with that of the domed church, resulting in a structure that was unique in medieval architecture.

opposite page
Interior of Piacenza Cathedral, circa 1122–1150

A trading junction on the route between Milan and Rimini, Piacenza showed its economic prosperity by rebuilding the cathedral after the earthquake of 1117; at the same time, it declared itself a free commune. The central nave and the chancel, covered by a sexpartite (six-celled) vault of French origin, express a sensibility that was new to Italy: the height of the pilasters and arcades gives the impression of a hall-like interior. The reliefs adorning the pilasters celebrate the arts and crafts guilds that had commissioned them. Combined with the new middle class, this was a demonstration of the importance given in art to the social transformations occurring at the time.

Narthex of Sant'Evasio Cathedral, Casale Monferrato, Italy, circa 1107

The narthex of the cathedral in Casale Monferrato opens out toward the main body of the church, a high and spacious rectangular hall covered by a single vault and surrounded on three sides by minor bays. The vault has a unique and innovative pattern deriving from the late Romanesque in Lombardy: flat, parallel ribs that intersect at right angles, like gigantic round arches, on which thin walls rise, connected by vaults reminiscent of Islamic stellar vaults. Such a high and broad space surrounded by minor spaces brings back the idea of the westwork in a completely original way.

BENEDETTO ANTELAMI

The work of Benedetto Antelami (1150–1230) was first documented in Parma in 1178 (the year he assisted on a pulpit project, from which a very playful slab, *The Deposition,* is the only surviving piece). He not only became one the most innovative figures in Romanesque Italian sculpture, but also one of its most original architects. Little is known of his life. He may have come from Lombardy, where works by a master called Antelami are now documented. He had in-depth knowledge of Greek and Roman architecture and of painting from antiquity, and his early training was completed in France, where he kept up-to-date with the artistic trends of the region. He may even have worked as an apprentice on the decorative sculpture of the Church of St Trophime in Arles. Some historians believe he went to Ile-de-France, where he would have come into contact with Gothic art. Between roughly 1180 and 1190, with the help of his workshop, he completed the sculptural decoration on the façade of the cathedral in Fidenza, where two free-standing statues of the prophets stand out, placed between niches near the central entrance portal. This type of monumental sculpture had not been seen since late antiquity, and Antelami drew on French sculpture from that era in order to apply monumentality and spontaneity to his work. A commemorative stone from 1196 attests to the beginning of decoration work on the baptistery at the cathedral in Parma, a project for which he was also the architect, and which is now his masterpiece.

opposite page
Façade of the Basilica of Sant'Andrea by Benedetto Antelami, Vercelli, Italy, 1219–1227

The façade of Sant'Andrea shows an exemplary fusion of Romanesque tradition and the new influences of the Gothic: Lombard-Emilian features such as the pitched roof, round-arch portals, horizontal string courses, openings in the side towers and double orders of arcades combined with Provençal and Norman elements, such as the deep, splayed portals, the side towers and their cusps, and the capitals with curling leaves. The ample rose window is located at the intersection of imaginary diagonals, dividing the façade in a rationally proportioned scheme. This serves to enhance the chromatic quality of the materials: the white of the plaster, the red of the brickwork and the green stone of the ribs.

The baptistery in Parma by Benedetto Antelami, begun 1196

The baptistery of Parma represents a unique fusion of architecture and sculpture, where a signature from the artist, Benedetto Antelami, in one of the portals confirms that work began in 1196. The octagonal building, which revives the plan of the early-Christian baptisteries, has six storeys, some with open galleries thanks to the use of Norman-style cavity walls (walls treated with tracery and internal galleries situated in front of the windows). The baptistery is famous for its sculptures, also by Antelami, while its monumental plan and the architrave in the blind arcades, at street level as well as in the four orders of loggias above, display unmistakable Classical influences.